MW00470690

The Samuel & Althea Stroum Lectures

IN JEWISH STUDIES

The
Kiss
of
God

*Spiritual and Mystical
Death in Judaism*

MICHAEL FISHBANE

UNIVERSITY OF WASHINGTON PRESS

Seattle & London

Copyright © 1994 by the University of Washington Press
Printed in the United States of America

All rights reserved. No part of this publication may be
reproduced or transmitted in any form or by any means,
electronic or mechanical, including photocopy, recording,
or any information storage or retrieval system, without
permission in writing from the publisher.

Library of Congress Cataloging-in-Publication Data
Fishbane, Michael A.
    The kiss of God : spiritual and mystical death in Judaism
/ by Michael Fishbane.
        p.   cm. – (The Samuel & Althea Stroum lectures
in Jewish studies)
    Includes bibliographical references and index.
    ISBN 0–295–97308–0
    1. Spiritual life – Judaism.   2. God (Judaism) – Worship
and love.   3. Yetzer hara (Judaism)   4. Death – Religious
aspects – Judaism.   5. Judaism – Doctrines.   I. Title.   II.
Series: Samuel and Althea Stroum lectures in Jewish studies.
BM723.F53   1994
296.7'1 – dc20   93–31394
                                                  CIP

The paper used in this publication meets the minimum
requirements of American National Standard
for Information Sciences – Permanence of Paper
for Printed Library Materials, ANSI Z39.48–1984.

The Samuel & Althea Stroum Lectures

IN JEWISH STUDIES

Samuel Stroum, businessman, community leader, and philanthropist, by a major gift to the Jewish Federation of Greater Seattle, established the Samuel and Althea Stroum Philanthropic Fund.

In recognition of Mr. and Mrs. Stroum's deep interest in Jewish history and culture, the Board of Directors of the Jewish Federation of Greater Seattle, in cooperation with the Jewish Studies Program of the Henry M. Jackson School of International Studies at the University of Washington, established an annual lectureship at the University of Washington known as the Samuel and Althea Stroum Lectureship in Jewish Studies. This lectureship makes it possible to bring to the area outstanding scholars and interpreters of Jewish thought, thus promoting a deeper understanding of Jewish history, religion, and culture. Such understanding can lead to an enhanced appreciation of the Jewish contributions to the historical and cultural traditions that have shaped the American nation.

The terms of the gift also provide for the publication from time to time of the lectures or other appropriate materials resulting from or related to the lectures.

For Elisha

Contents

Preface

I had been pondering the theme of mystical death in Judaism for some time, and so it was a welcome opportunity to receive an invitation to deliver the Samuel and Althea Stroum Lectures in Jewish Studies at the University of Washington for 1990. I offer my sincere thanks to Professor Hillel Kieval, director of the Jewish Studies Program, and to his colleagues and staff for many kindnesses extended to me during my stay in Seattle. The initial lectures were rethought in the course of a seminar delivered at the University of Chicago and completely rewritten and expanded thereafter. I have tried nevertheless to preserve both the oral style of the original presentation and the balance of emphasis given there. Thus although the present format permits a more nuanced and developed treatment than the lectures allowed, the fact that I consider themes and topics in Jewish sources covering nearly two thousand years has led me (in most instances) to make a certain selection of examples and (largely) to forgo a comparative perspective. Naturally, where necessary or instructive, Stoic, Neoplatonic, or Sufic influences on Jewish sources have been indicated; but detailed parallels with Christian, Islamic, or even Eastern traditions are either omitted or relegated to brief notes. Because many of the Jewish texts and thematics of this subject have never been collected or analyzed in monograph form, I have thought it best to maintain such a singular focus overall. This orientation also accords with my conviction that an internal phenomenology and comparison are the necessary first part of any comparative work done in the history of religions.

Preface

As always, the love and care of my dear Mona have nurtured my work from beginning to end. My thanks are bound up with our shared life. In addition, I am very grateful to my friends Professors Arthur Green, Zeev Gries, Moshe Idel, and Yehuda Liebes for their reactions to and comments on this work; their shared passion for this theme and our common concerns were expressed in many personal and professional ways. The probing curiosity of my students has also helped me to clarify several points – and I am most appreciative. In its final stages the manuscript received the devoted care of my secretary, Mrs. Peggy Edwards. Her conscientious professional work and gracious personal assistance have left me very much in her debt. Warm thanks also to Mr. Michael Terry of the Asher Library at Spertus College for fulfilling many odd and urgent requests with gracious efficiency.

The most precious pleasure associated with this book came in conversations with my son Elisha Reuven on the occasion of his becoming a Bar Mitzvah in Jerusalem, on 10 Tammuz, 5751 (*Parashat Ḥuqqat*). Not only did he choose the biblical verse "Let him kiss me with the kisses of his mouth" (Songs 1:2) to inscribe his invitation, out of his own clear understanding of spiritual love and our many talks on it, but he entered deeply into the thematics of life and death that recur in the scriptural readings he prepared. Studying the commentaries and integrating them in an original way, his soul flew – transformed like the dove's wings of Elisha in rabbinic lore. It is therefore a father's joy to dedicate this book to him in love, beyond all death.

'Erev Shavu'ot, 5752

The Kiss of God

Spiritual and Mystical
Death in Judaism

Introduction

At the heart of the Hebrew Bible is the great exhortation found in Deuteronomy 6:5, "you shall love the Lord your God with all your heart and with all your soul and with all your might." These words are also at the heart of Judaism and constitute its religious ideal. The people are addressed with this positive duty following Moses' proclamation that "the Lord is One," unique and alone (v. 4). In the legal vocabulary of ancient Israel the term "love" formally stipulates loyalty and covenantal commitment.[1] But what more is involved?

The language is telling. First and foremost, the speech articulates a spiritual task for each and every individual ("you *shall* love"). A personal response to the communal creed is thus required; and the terms of this response are specified in the deepest and most comprehensive way ("with all your heart and with all your soul and with all your might"). Clearly, the language of love evokes more than legal loyalty. It claims the total self. The triple formula "with all" punctuates the absolute nature of this demand, and each phrase determines a distinct mode of devotion. In view of our limited understanding of biblical psychology, the sequence of heart, soul, and might may even mark a particular intensification of personal commitment: beginning with one's heart (or mind), expanding to one's soul (or life force), and culminating with one's entire self as a locus of energy (or might).[2] Such a reading of the list moves from part to whole and complements another that would see here a progression from inner state (thought and emotion) to outer effect (or worldly

3

Introduction

production).[3] Whatever the case, the overall intent is clear. An exclusive God demands absolute devotion.

As heirs of biblical Scripture, the ancient rabbis turned to Deuteronomy 6:4 as the primary formulation of their monotheistic faith and regarded the duty to "love the Lord your God with all your heart and with all your soul and with all your might" (6:5) as an uncompromising challenge. They therefore turned the text this way and that for exegetical clues that might delineate the nature and extent of the task. Not surprisingly, the conflicts of classical rabbinic psychology are discovered in their interpretations along with the highest ideals of spiritual perfection. A brief exploration of these interpretations will provide a useful prologue to the religious agenda to be considered in subsequent chapters.

One of the earliest comments on Deuteronomy 6:5 is found in the Mishnah, *Berakhot* IX.5. Here, after citing the entire verse, each phrase is successively repeated and explained. It begins: "*with all your heart* – with your two inclinations, with the good inclination [*yetzer*] and with the evil inclination [*yetzer*]."[4] At first glance, the comment is puzzling and seems entirely arbitrary. But this is not so. The understanding of the human heart as comprising two distinct inclinations was a well-established feature of ancient Jewish psychology. Its origin derives from such scriptural passages as Genesis 8:21, where we read that "the *yetzer* of the heart [*leb*] of a human being is evil from his youth," as well as from other traditions. Among these one may count certain metaphysical speculations concerning "two ways" (good and evil) found in Jewish Hellenistic writings[5] and in moral dicta and midrashim of the sages,[6] as well as the connection drawn in the Dead Sea Scrolls between the dual "spirits" of human nature and the divinely determined nature of things.[7] The rabbis

4

drew on such ideas in their effort to characterize the inner conflicts of the religious person. With little difficulty they found support for their views in Scripture. Our text is a case in point. Starting from the deuteronomic exhortation to love God "with all your heart [*lebabekha*]," the sages noted that the letter bet (*b*) is doubled in the key word. Since this is not the case in the Genesis passage (which only mentions the evil *yetzer*), they drew the exegetical implication that the noun *lebabekha* encodes reference to *both* inclinations.[8]

But what is the meaning of this teaching? How can one love God with "two inclinations"? One possibility, urged by the sages, is for the true devotee to sublimate base instincts to divine ends. The clash of opposing *yetzer*s would of course still remain, but the negative effects of the evil inclination would be overcome. Such a religious psychology strikingly softens the stern duality of two opposing *yetzer*s and suggests the possibility of self-mastery. Justified or not, an even stronger strain of psychological optimism conditions the exegesis found in *Sifrei Deuteronomy* 32.[9] After citing the mishnaic exegesis, this midrashic source goes on to reread the crucial noun *lebabekha* as two words, *leb bakh*. In this way Moses is made to urge the people to love God "with every heart within you"[10] – or, perhaps, "with your whole heart." If we follow the first possibility, the meaning conforms to the interpretation of two hearts and would counsel using the evil *yetzer* in loving service of God. But I am more inclined to the second alternative ("with your whole heart"), in view of the explication that follows: "that your heart not be divided [*ḥaluq*] toward God." From this it would seem that the instruction is to love God with a perfect service and not be conflicted.[11] The divided self must be brought in line, for the One God demands all one's heart.

Introduction

The second demand of Scripture is equally absolute. According to the Mishnah, the duty of loving God "with all your soul" means "even if He takes your soul." Love of God is thus a total commitment – unto death. To reinforce this point, the commentary in the *Tosefta*[12] and *Sifrei* supplement the Mishnah with a biblical verse (from Psalm 44:23) often cited in martyrological contexts: "For Your sake we are killed all day long (and regarded as sheep for the slaughter)."[13] At first sight, this passage merely seconds the point – and has the merit of complementing the Torah text ("*all* day long"; "*all* your soul"). But on closer inspection the Psalms testimony is odd. Although it articulates the people's claim that they die for God's sake, the locution is extreme. Surely no one (including the psalmist) would think to take the hyperbole literally – unless there was another purpose in mind.

It would thus appear that Rabbi Simeon ben Menasia must have had an ulterior motive when he took the words at face value and posed the ensuing query in the *Sifrei*. "Now is it really possible for a person to die *all day long*?" Put this way the interjection has no answer. The sage knows this, of course, and surely meant the question as a rhetorical prelude to his own solution: "[Thus this Scripture] can only mean that the Holy One, blessed be He, regards the righteous as if they are killed every day." At first glance, this answer seems merely to replace the hyperbole with a pious nostrum. For what can it mean? And how does it explicate the first half of the verse (where the psalmist says that he is "killed all day long")? We must approach the answer in stages. The first clue lies in the phrase "we are regarded as sheep for the slaughter." From his explanation, it is clear that Rabbi Simeon has reinterpreted the passage in a complex manner. First of all, he understands God to be the implied subject of the

Introduction

verb "regarded" (i.e., "we are regarded *by God*"), so that the verb takes on a specific theological resonance; second, he reinterprets the particle "as," so that it does not mark a simile but a hypothetical comparison ("as if"); and finally, he applies both revisions (in the second phrase) to the opening words. The result is a transformation of the martyrological ideal – a routinization of it, so to speak – such that the righteous are considered by God as if they die daily. But what is it about the righteous or their behavior that connects them to dying? Just what does Rabbi Simeon mean? A roughly contemporary tradition found in the Babylonian Talmud (*b. Berakhot* 61*b*) is instructive in this regard:

It has been taught: Rabbi Yosi the Galilean says, "The righteous are ruled [lit., judged] by their good inclination, as [Scripture] says, 'For I am poor and needy, and my heart is slain [*ḥalal*] within me' [Psalm 109:22]; the wicked are ruled by their evil inclination, as it says, 'Transgression speaks to the wicked, "In my heart there is no fear of God"' [Psalm 36:2]; [and] average persons are ruled by both inclinations, as it says, 'For it stands to the right of the needy, to save him from those who would rule [or condemn] him'" [Psalm 109:31].

In this teaching, each type of person (righteous, wicked, and average) is characterized by a distinct relationship to the good and evil inclinations: the righteous are ruled by the first, the wicked by the second, and average people by both. So far, this division is unexceptional. And it would remain so, were it not for the proof texts appended to explicate the types, for these sources go beyond the formulaic dictum and reveal the dynamic complexity of the rabbinic psychology of two *yetzers*. Thus the citation

7

Introduction

from Psalm 36:2 makes use of an internal quotation in order to dramatize the rebellious heart of the wicked person. Indeed, the "transgression" functions there as a personified introjection of the evil inclination, substantivized as the "heart" that denies the divine dimension. By contrast, the citation from Psalm 109:22 speaks of the righteous man as having humbled himself and "killed" his evil "heart."[14] This strong language suggests an act of mortification, some sacrifice of base desire for God's sake. Accordingly, if one regards martyrdom as the acceptance of death in extremis for the love of God (the first midrashic interpretation), killing one's evil *yetzer* may correspondingly function as the daily exaction of such supreme devotion. Psychological strife thus provides the drama of personal perfection, and slaying the evil inclination is the perpetual combat whereby the devotee offers "all" his soul to God.[15] This is the new interpretation of love unto death offered by Rabbi Simeon ben Menasia.

The preceding passages help frame our inquiry. They reveal a Judaism focused on the Bible, as interpreted and extended by the sages. With respect to the duty to love God found in Deuteronomy 6:5, the worshipper is exhorted to struggle with the competing inclinations which make up human nature. Success is marked by the vigorous ascendance of the good *yetzer,* through the active devotion of "all" one's heart and soul to God, even unto death. Such self-sacrifice marks a life of this-worldly asceticism. That is, the religious individual is urged to resolve the conflictual nature of the self through self-control and uncompromising devotion to divine service. The split in the self (between the good and evil *yetzer*s) is thus a measure of the split between the self and God. Tradition is crucial here, for it specifies the redeeming tasks of love. In comparative terms, such behavior constitutes an activist mode of individual salvation in the here and now.

The conflict of inclinations within the self was also imagined as a conflict between the soul and the body. In such cases the good *yetzer* was often portrayed as physically confined, like a person in prison. This image recalls Plato's punning comparison of the body (*soma*) to a prison (*sema*). He worked this play to good effect in his own (philosophical) version of the salvation of the soul. And it was largely due to the influence of his thought that the image entered Jewish religious philosophy. But the motif had roots in rabbinic Midrash as well. The following parable from the *Avot de-Rabbi Nathan* (I.xvi.32*a*) is indicative and further illumines the drama of inclinations so crucial to medieval doctrines of personal salvation.[16]

The evil inclination is [like] a king over 248 parts of the body. When a person goes to perform [the divine] commandments, all his bodily parts become indolent because the evil inclination is king over 248 parts of a person's body. By contrast, the good inclination is only like one confined to prison [*bet ha-'asurim*]; as it is said [in Scripture]: "For out of prison [*bet ha-surim*] he came forth to be king [Ecclesiastes 4:14]. This refers to the good inclination.

By virtue of a double analogy, two kings are contrasted: the evil inclination, which rules the body now; and the good inclination, which will ultimately prevail. This temporal tension is structured by spatial imagery. The two are not symmetrical, but the overall effect is. In the first case, the evil inclination is within the body and inhibits the good inclination's desire to perform God's service.[17] This is an image of internal power and control, entirely fitting classical Judaic notions. By contrast, the

Introduction

good inclination is portrayed as a prisoner who comes forth to be king. Here the figure of release predominates and presents an image of external control and freedom more befitting Hellenic notions. But once joined, these analogies work together. The point of the preacher is that the present constraints of the evil inclination will one day end, and the temporary inhibitions of the good inclination will cease. On that day, one will worship God wholeheartedly. Or in the (reinterpreted) words of Ecclesiastes, at present the good inclination is confined to the prison house (*bet ha-'asurim*) of the body, hemmed in by the sins (*ha-'asurim;* lit., "the prohibitions") performed while turning (*surim*) from God; but in time to come the captive will be set free and rule the body for the glory of God. By substituting the good inclination for the soul, the preacher has refigured a Greek image of philosophical salvation into the language of Jewish religious psychology. It remained for a later synthesis (in the Middle Ages) to restore the soul to its rightful place. Then the soul's release from bodily constraints became an authentic sign of spiritual perfection – of an attachment to God beyond the hold of the material world. In this life, even a moment of such bliss was sufficient.

In a remarkable prayer for the Day of Atonement, Rabbi Yehuda Halevi (ca. 1085–1141) gave poignant expression to this yearning – and its frustrations.[18] "How can I serve my Maker while I am still a prisoner of passion and slave to desire?" This cry of spiritual despair turns on an ancient conflict, embedded in paradoxical puns: service of God (*'e'evod*) is juxtaposed to slavery (*'eved*), and the divine Maker (*yotzri*) is contrasted with the evil inclination (*yitzri*).[19] Moreover, the self feels bound, a prisoner (*'asir*) of his *yetzer*, which "hounds" him "like an enemy from youth."[20] This allusion to Genesis 8:21

Introduction

("the *yetzer* of the heart of a human being is evil from his youth") darkens earlier references to youthful pleasure, even as the reference to captivity (*'asir*) reinforces an earlier appeal that God "restore me from the prison house [*ma'asar*] of folly."

But the most poignant section of the prayer for divine aid comes at the beginning. Here Halevi confesses his consummate desire for God's grace. He would gladly die, he says; for life without God "is death."

> O Lord! all my desire is toward You,
> even if it does not rise to speech.
> Grant me Your favor a mere moment –
> and I would die.
> Please grant my wish, and I will commit
> my spirit to Your keeping.
> I would sleep, and my sleep be sweet.
> For when I am far from You –
> my life is death;
> And were I to cleave to You –
> my death would be life!
> But I don't know what to do,
> what I should bring You in service.

The seeker wants God above all else; he wants the grace of divine favor. To be far from God, he says, is a living death; whereas nearness, even for a moment, is a dying into true life. This paradox will engage us later on. For now let me simply underscore the transvaluation of values involved. For Halevi and similar seekers, life in this world is a torment of false desire, a web of entanglements in which the face of pleasure is the receding image of God. Only the death of these drives, by the grace of God, will give life. For his part the poet offers "all" his desires to God, in an act of commitment reminiscent of midrashic

Introduction

readings of Deuteronomy 6:5. The irony is profound. By an ingenious pun Halevi takes the noun *ta'avah,* used later in the prayer to indicate unruly urges ("slave to desire"), and employs it to mean both hopeful longing and the full thrust of spiritual passion.[21] All this is given to God in a spontaneous speech-act. But when instinct turns to thought ("But I don't know what to do"), the torment returns. The stanza ends in anguish.

Let me sum up, and thereby indicate the overall shape of this book. Two broad concerns recur: the longing for spiritual transcendence, through overcoming material desire; and the longing for physical transcendence, through spiritual devotion of the body to God. The first involves the tumultuous struggle with the evil inclination, which must be ruled (through religious practice and willpower) in order that the divine spirit or soul may be truly free. That freedom will result initially in pure and devoted worship and eventually in higher flights of the soul to God. The perfected soul will thus enjoy moments of bliss in this life and ultimate felicity in the world to come. Philosophers and mystics articulate this point differently, just as each values certain practices over others. But both agree that a life imprisoned by desire is a living death and that dying into God (by total self-sacrifice) is the only true life. Modes and motifs of this dying will be the concern of chapter 1.

If loving God "with all your heart" involves the spiritual perfection of the inner self, loving God "with all your soul" involves (according to tradition) the readiness to sacrifice the body as a martyr. This requires physical transcendence, plain and simple. Judaism saw this act as the supreme expression of sanctification and commitment and cultivated martyrdom as an ideal for thought

Introduction

and deed. In fact, where circumstances precluded dying for God's sake, meditations and ritual practices were substituted. Thus one might spiritually undergo a dying to God ("with all your soul") while alive by repeatedly dying to selfish desires with every devoted performance of the commandments. Some modes and motifs of this martyrological death (both real and imagined) will be discussed in chapter 2.

Chapter 3 will blend themes of the preceding discussions and focus on the ritualization of spiritual death in Judaism. By this I mean those various practices, developed over centuries, which allow the worshipper to "die" mentally and physically (through meditation and simulation) during the daily liturgy. These actions provided a training in perfection to enable one to be wholeheartedly devoted to God – in normal and, God forbid, in extreme circumstances. The task was to internalize thoroughly the duty to "love the Lord your God with all your heart and with all your soul." Anything else gave honor to the self, and not God alone. [22]

Judaism thus puts the demand to love God at the center of its ritual life and has variously explained that demand through interpretation. The preceding pages provide a glimpse of this fact. In all, Judaism is a vast intertextual system whose internal life expands and contracts through exegesis. This is the secret of its spirit; and this is the reason that even the love of God in Judaism is *an interpreted love*. Only tradition can tell the faithful how to love truly. But only the living God can confirm the quest. Perhaps that is why the seeker cries so longingly, "[Oh] let Him kiss me with the kisses of His mouth!" This longing lies at the heart of this book.

"If you wish to live, then die"
Aspects of Death
and Desire in
Jewish Spirituality

In the great love song of the Hebrew Bible, Solomon's
Song of Songs, the female beloved has the first word.
Yishaqeni mi-nishiqot pihu, she cries to her friends: "Let
him kiss me with the kisses of his mouth" (1:2). And
then, in a more private reverie, she speaks to the lover in
her heart and says: "For your love is sweeter than wine."
With these words, the woman confesses the hope of love
and its consummate joy. She is at once ready for erotic
fulfillment (symbolized here by the kiss) and convinced
that this rapture exceeds all earthly delights (symbolized
by wine, that old elixir of physical desire). Similar tropes
of wish fulfillment and comparison suffuse the Song,
whether in the language of "seeking" and "finding"
(3:1–4), which dramatize the temporal deferments of love,
or in the form of simile and synecdoche, which displace
the physical energy of love throughout the natural world.
Ever-new images thus conjugate the rhythms of eros
with the arousals of nature – giving figural expression,
we might say, to the repeated quest of the lovers for
fulfillment. And so, when the initial figures of kissing
and wine recur near the end of the Song (8:1–2), they tend

to mark the renewal of hope and desire. All-consuming, "love is as fierce as death" and stoked by a divine-like fire (8:6). Nothing can quench it (8:7).

But it can be transfigured, as we see from the bold interpretation of the Song that dominates ancient rabbinic culture. Thanks go first to Solomon, not for writing a mere song, a song of physical love between two lovers, but a Song of Songs, a most superior song about the covenantal love between God and Israel.[1] According to the sages, Solomon was inspired to render the sacred history of Israel found in the Torah into poetic images for the people.[2] Through metaphor and simile, he transfigured earthly eros into tropes of tradition and memory – though it remained for the rabbis to recover this historical sense through parables and figures of their own. The results are found in assorted passages in the Talmud and midrashic literature, in the Aramaic paraphrase used in the synagogue, and in the grand anthology known as *Song of Songs Rabba*. Whoever would know more than Scripture tells, let him turn to the tropes of Midrash and be wise, for here the sages do not simply recount the events of the Exodus or Sinai, but much more, on the basis of hints found in Solomon's Song. Do not simply read "like a mare among Pharaoh's steeds I imagined you, my beloved" (Songs 1:9), but rather learn how God himself appeared, or seemed to appear, to Israel at the Sea;[3] and do not think that the cry to "let him kiss me with the kisses of his mouth" (1:2) is mere erotic desire, but come and hear how God spoke the commandments at Sinai and how Israel was kissed for their willing acceptance of each and every word.[4]

The rabbis thus place the Exodus and, particularly, the events at Sinai at the center of their national reading of the Song. In addition to those traditions that use the

Death and Desire in Jewish Spirituality

image of the kiss to indicate the intimacy of the event at Sinai, another cluster records its utter terror.[5] For now the revealed words of the Decalogue strike death in the hearts of the people.

Rabbi Joshua ben Levi said: "At each and every word which issued from the mouth of the Holy One, blessed be He, the soul of Israel departed, as it is said, 'My soul departed when he spoke' [Songs 5:6]. But when their soul departed after the first commandment, how did they receive the second commandment? He brought down the dew that will resurrect the dead in the future and resurrected them, as it is said, 'A bountiful rain You released, O God'" [Psalm 68:10].[6]

To arrive at this interpretation, Rabbi Joshua made two ingenious moves. First, he linked the rabbinic word *dibber* (word, commandment) to the phrase "when he spoke" (*be-dabbero*) in Songs 5:6, and thus he transformed the bated breath of earthly passion into the death scene of supernatural revelation. His second exegetical act was to construe the phrase "when he spoke" as a continuous divine event (i.e., "whenever He spoke") and infuse the old rabbinic tradition of resurrecting dew into Psalm 68:10 – a verse that is preceded by a reference to Sinai (v. 9) and followed by the phrase "the Lord gives a command" (v. 12). In this way, the Ten Commandments were imparted to the people through a succession of deaths and rebirths.[7]

According to another version, the death and revival of the people at the opening word, "I am the Lord your God" (Exodus 20:2), immediately follow an account of Moses' perception of the supernal spectrum in the highest heaven and the people's direct vision of God's Glory enthroned in the highest heaven.[8] "Immediately, the souls of the *righteous* expired." To prevent a recurrence of this

16

event, after the miraculous rebirth each of the 600,000 souls present was assigned to the care of two angels: one raised his ward's head, so that he would continue to encounter God "face to face"; and the other clasped the human's breast, so that his heart would not escape. From this sequel, it would seem that the death of "the righteous" is a national event; but given their vision of God's Glory, which the prophet Ezekiel later saw upon the Heavenly Chariot (Ezekiel 1:25–26), it would also seem that this account of the Sinai revelation has been infused with mystical motifs.[9] The death scene is thereby transposed. Although the deadly danger of God's presence remains, it now hints of a collective rapture – a death in ecstasy, so prevalent in Jewish sources. We shall trace these developments below.

For the present, it is first necessary to introduce another motif associated with the divine kiss: the death of the righteous. Its popular locus is a tradition preserved in the Talmud (*b. Baba Bathra* 17a). We learn there that "our rabbis taught: there are six [persons] over whom the Angel of Death had no dominion – Abraham, Isaac, and Jacob, Moses, Aaron, and Miriam." Justification for including the Patriarchs makes use of assorted biblical passages and spiritual allusions. They are beside the point here. But with respect to the three others, we learn that "it is written in connection with them [that they died] *by the mouth of the Lord.*" Clearly, the reference is to Numbers 33:38 and Deuteronomy 34:5 (referring to the deaths of Aaron and Moses, respectively); and most cleverly, the (anonymous) sages midrashically construe the standard idiom '*al pi*, "at the command of," in an utterly literal way in order to support the idea of death "by the mouth" of God. The mysterious death of these persons by divine dictate (in Scripture) is thus anthropomorphically transfigured in this midrash. What is more, the very moment of death is itself infused with an erotic dimension. The sages were not unaware of this, for the Talmud goes on to raise the obvious point: "But the words 'by the mouth of the Lord' are not found in connection with [the death of] Miriam." To this apparent conflict Rabbi Eleazar made an intriguing rebuttal: "Miriam also died by a kiss, as we learn from the occurrence of the word 'there' [both with regard to her death] and that of Moses [Numbers 20:1; Deuteronomy 34:5]. And why is it not said [more directly] of her that [she died] *by the mouth* of the Lord?' – Because such an expression would be disrespectful [to her, as a pious woman]." The erotic issue is thus raised and elided by a hermeneutical legerdemain. The tradition in *Song of Songs Rabba* (1.2.xvi) goes on to ask how we can further learn that not only these saints but all the righteous die by the kiss; and it answers: "for it is written: 'Let him kiss me with the kiss*es* of his mouth.'" The plural proves the point.

What is particularly striking about these traditions is that death by divine kiss is a sign of special favor, a mark of grace given to the saintly. Indeed, as the full passage in *Songs Rabba* makes clear, this is particularly the reward granted to the most faithful adherents of the norms and ideals of rabbinic Judaism – the sages themselves. Compared with the Sinai episode (and this midrash uses the two motifs to frame its many comments on Songs 1:2), the rapturous death of the righteous by God culminates a lifetime of spiritual labor, of studying the Law and observing the commandments. The paragon of such perfection was Moses himself, and in a series of medieval legends known as *Peṭirat Moshe* (The Death of Moses), the death scene by God's kiss is exalted to the pinnacle of a saintly life. [10] A striking midrashic account is found in *Deuteronomy Rabba* 11.x. Mirroring the legend of Moses' vaunted ascension past the angels to receive the Torah in the heavenly realms, the angels now descend to earth at God's command to end the life of this righteous one. But Moses foils his foe with thrusts of the Law, necessitating divine intervention. In one poignant scene, near the end, Moses' soul refuses to leave his saintly body, perfected by the commandments and celibate since Sinai. But no creature born of woman can live forever, and God withdraws the soul by a kiss. Thus does Moses die "by the mouth of the Lord," a death whose erotic overtones resound. Indeed, in this episode Moses is (metonymically) feminized through identity with his soul, so that the climax is a transcendental union of opposites. As we shall see, this theme recurs in Jewish philosophical sources. More popularly, the motif of Moses' death by divine kiss was also kept alive in the religious poetry of the synagogue. The annual recitation of Deuteronomy 34 in the liturgical cycle, as well as on Moses' "*Jahrzeit*" on the Seventh of Adar, was a favorite occasion for the bards.[11]

In this and other ways, the thematics of *Songs Rabba* penetrated later generations. Most influential are the individualization of the kiss of God and its benefaction to the righteous for their deeds in this world. The kiss is thus the culmination of a spiritual quest, a rapture of the perfected soul into divine bliss. Several puns underscore the point. These too are found in the Midrash, where the verb *yishaqeni*, "let him kiss me," is heard to hint at the soul's purification and cleaving to God. In the first case, the play is on the phrase *ke-mashaq gevim* in Isaiah 33:4, which is made to indicate the "joining of cisterns" for ritual immersion;[12] in the second, "the sound of the wings of the [heavenly] beasts [which support the Throne] touching [*mashiqot*] each other" (Ezekiel 3:13) is understood to convey the eros of mystical contact. Not all later traditions link the kiss of God with spiritual cleaving to God, some stressing only the one theme or the other. But their fusion in *Songs Rabba,* through a pun on the verb *yishaqeni* (kiss; cleave), indicates the complex template that later philosophical and mystical traditions could utilize. The further association of these topics with spiritual death entwines *eros* and *thanatos* in intricate ways. For the religious seeker, the quest for true life requires death of some sort. The precise nature of this death, and how it may be achieved, are the lessons of the masters.

The desire for death torments the God-intoxicated soul; for only in death (spiritual or physical) is there release from the earthly *yetzer* and absolute devotion to God. This yearning for spiritual connection drives Halevi and other Jewish Neoplatonists. But the philosophical roots of this offshoot settle in Hellenic antiquity, with Plato himself. Here we first find a distinction between natural and supernatural death, between the release of the body from the soul and the release of the soul from the body. The first is the common, all-too-human way of mortal decay; whereas the second is the unique way of the philosopher, who struggles with his passions that his soul may come in contact with divine Wisdom in this life and attain pure knowledge after death.[13] In the *Phaedo* we are taught:

The philosopher desires death. . . . What is the nature of that death which he desires? Death is the separation of soul and body – and the philosopher desires such a separation. He would like to be freed from the domination of the bodily pleasures of the senses, which are always perturbing his mental vision. . . . All the evils and impurities and necessities

of men come from the body. . . . Why then should he repine
when the hour of separation arrives? Why, if he is dead while
he lives, should he fear that other death, through which
alone he can behold Wisdom in her purity? (*Phaedo* 64–68;
B. Jowett translation)

The process of "practicing death," as Socrates says,
involves a progressive mental dissociation from the body
and a focus on divine truth. In Jewish Hellenism such
ideas were developed by Philo of Alexandria. Repeatedly,
he teaches that "the soul be purged of its passions and
distempers and infirmities and every viciousness of word
and deed."[14] And in a remarkable reading of the Nadab
and Abihu episode (Leviticus 10:1–2), these sons of Aaron
the priest are understood to have "stripped themselves" of
"passion and bodily constraint" and "drawn nigh to God"
in spiritual ecstasy.[15] "It is thus that Nadab and Abihu
die in order that they might live, receiving an incorruptible
life in exchange for mortal existence."[16]

A rabbinic version of this Greek virtue of spiritual death
for the sake of true life occurs in the Babylonian Talmud
(*Tamid* 32a). There, Alexander the Great, tutee of the
school of Aristotle and patron of Hellenic values, is said
to have come before the Jewish scholars of the south for
instruction. Among a series of queries and retorts reflecting Stoic piety, he asks, "What should a man do *in order
that he might live?*" And they reportedly answered, "He
should mortify [*yamit;* lit., "kill"] himself." Whereupon
Alexander asked, "What should a man do in order to die?"
To which question the Jewish sages replied, "He should
vivify himself"; that is, he should indulge in bodily desires.
These questions and all the others put by Alexander in *b.*
Tamid 31b–32a are missing in the medieval Hebrew version of the Alexander romance, *Sefer Toledot Aleksandros*

Death and Desire in Jewish Spirituality

ha-Makdoni, by Immanuel ben Jacob Bonfils. [17] But a great irony is thereby lost, for in the talmudic episode the leader of Hellenism learns Greek philosophical virtues from the rabbis. Or so it seems – for the sages do not counsel suppression of the evil *yetzer,* but death to the "beastly passions." The fact that they choose a formulation which echoes an idiom used by Philo, and which conforms to Greek philosophical piety more broadly, is itself telling. Indeed, the further fact that Ḥunayn ibn Isḥaq later quotes the dictum "Pursue death, and you will live" in the name of Socrates suggests that the talmudic dialogue (and Philo's remark) drew on ancient epitomes of the *Phaedo* in the school of Plato. [18] In any event, the rabbinic advice shows up in a medieval citation by Jonah Gerondi (*Sha'arei Teshuva* II.17) of the old ethical tractate *Derekh Eretz*: "If it be your will not to die, die before you die [*mut 'ad shelo tamut*]." [19] The same idiom recurs in Sufic sources and even in a prayer by St. John of the Cross:

> Vivo sin vivir en mí
> y de tal manera espero,
> que muero porque no muero.
>
> I live without life in me –
> and by such a way hope
> that I die because I do not die. [20]

But let us return to the Jewish–Greek synthesis. Beginning with Philo, though derived from Plato, its focus is on a mode of ascetical piety that sets itself against this-worldly desires, precisely because these desires stimulate the physical self and turn one away from God and spiritual deliverance. As a mode of intellectual activism, such piety advocates a kind of self-liberation of the soul through a strengthening of the intellect and its attachment to wisdom. This point is made with exegetical sharpness by the earliest Jewish Neoplatonic philosopher, Isaac Israeli. In his tenth-century work *The Book of Definitions,* he provides the following quotation and commentary.

Plato said that philosophy is a zeal, a striving, and concern for death. Says Isaac: This is a description of great profundity and elevated meaning. For in saying "concern for death" the sage meant it to be understood in the sense of the killing of beastly desires and lusts, for in their mortification and avoidance is the highest rank, the supernal splendor and the entry into the realm of truth. And by vivifying beastly desires and lusts and by strengthening them, men of intellect are drawn away from that which is due to God in the way of obedience, purity, and attention to prayer at the prescribed hours.[21]

This is a wonderful piece of synthetic exegesis, blending Greek and Jewish thought in a commentary form. Israeli gives Plato (not revelation) the voice of authority summarizing just that section of the *Phaedo* (64–68) quoted earlier. To this he glosses, in his own voice, his own epitome from the Talmud (*b. Tamid* 32*a*): that "the killing" of beastly desires leads to the highest good, whereas "vivifying beastly desires" draws one from the true path. Accordingly, the scholars of the south rescue old Plato from obscurity – and Isaac Israeli has not merely adjusted a Hellenized Jewish teaching to Platonic thought, he has Platonized that instruction to boot. Thus, proper praxis requires mental discipline and self-control. But that is not all. A glance at the conclusion shows that Israeli also speaks as a committed Jew, dedicated to the regimen of the Law as a discipline of self-development. Indeed, by referring to "the way of obedience, purity, and attention to prayer at the prescribed hours," there is another decisive tilt: from the lonely path of the philosopher to the communal path of the people. Blending solitary virtues with Halakhah – the philosophical quest with political solidarity – marks the way of Moses with a toga.

Maimonides (1135–1204) continues this philosophical tradition. Although his great work *The Guide of the Perplexed* is suffused with a concern for individual perfection (with the "governance of the solitary," as Shem Ṭov designates it²²), comments there and in the compendious *Mishneh Torah* make clear that for the "Great Eagle" halakhic practice is the divinely given means whereby one's soul may be attached to God in this world and permanently joined to the Active Intellect upon death. The desires of material existence are thus controlled by ritual piety and diminished by philosophical knowledge. In a sense, there is in Maimonides' doctrine a kind of idealism by which you are or become what you think about; so that to be intellectually focused upon God at all times is progressively to strengthen the link between the human intellect and its divine source. But such a bond can never be complete so long as the soul remains in the body, and the merest trace of matter taints it with an earthly hue. To be perfected one must love God with an undivided spiritual attention ("with all your soul") throughout life. The climax, for Maimonides, is death: death by a divine kiss. Here is how he describes it in a famous passage near the end of the *Guide* (III. 51).

[I]n the measure in which the faculties of the body are weakened and the fire of the desires is quenched, the intellect is strengthened . . . its apprehension is purified, and it rejoices in what it apprehends. The result is that when a perfect man is stricken with years and approaches death, this apprehension increases very powerfully, joy over this apprehension becomes stronger, until the soul is separated from the body at that moment in this state of pleasure. Because of this the Sages have indicated with reference to the deaths of Moses, Aaron and Miriam that the three of them died by a kiss. They said that the dictum, "And Moses the servant of the Lord died there in the land of Moab by the mouth of the Lord" (Deuteronomy 34:5), indicates that he died by the kiss. Similarly it is said of Aaron: "By the mouth of the Lord, and died there" (Numbers 33:38). And they said of Miriam in the same way: "She also died by the kiss." But with regard to her it is not said, "by the mouth of the Lord"; because she was a woman, the use of the figurative expression was not suitable with regard to her. Their purpose was to indicate that the three of them died in the pleasure of this apprehension due to the intensity of passionate love. In this dictum the Sages, may their memory be blessed, followed the generally accepted poetical way of expression that calls the apprehension that is achieved in a state of intense and passionate love for Him, may He be exalted, a kiss, in accordance with the dictum: "Let him kiss me with the kisses of his mouth" (Songs 1:2). . . . After having reached this condition of enduring permanence, that intellect remains in one and the same state, the impediment that sometimes screened him off having been removed. And he will remain in that state of intense pleasure, which does not belong to the genus of bodily pleasures, as we have explained.[23]

In this remarkable discussion, Maimonides interprets an interpretation of Scripture in terms of a spiritual death in rapture. The sequence is as follows. The old rabbinical sages (in the Talmud and Midrash) read the accounts of the death of Moses and Aaron "by the mouth of the Lord" quite literally. For them this expression does not simply refer to death by divine direction, which is the apparent plain sense of the passage, but death "by the kiss of God." The righteous thus die peacefully, they taught; and their souls are withdrawn from their bodies as painlessly as a hair is removed from milk (*b. Berakhot* 8a). But Maimonides went further when he interpreted this expiration as a death in ecstasy, a death "in the pleasure of [intellectual] apprehension due to the intensity of passionate love." The kiss is thus "a poetical way" of talking about the consummation of spiritual *eros* as the death of the earthly self. He has thus allegorized Songs 1:2, "Let him kiss me with the kisses of his mouth." Perhaps for the first time, we now have a personal reading of the Song – one that takes the personal language seriously but avoids its lyrical lust. To dodge this danger, earlier commentators from the rabbinic sages to Rashi resolutely adopted a historical reading (noted earlier). Maimonides converts it. For him "the fire of the desires is quenched" – but not true love (cf. Songs 8:7). Driven by the purification of apprehension and the joy it engenders, the intellect strengthens its bond with God. It is finally released by a kiss. However "poetical," death is thus eroticized as a transcendental pleasure of "enduring permanence." Indeed, with exquisite irony the original earth-centered *eros* is transfigured, and the male–female love of the Song is now read as God (spiritually) kissing men but not women, for that would be a consummate breach of propriety.

By the thirteenth century, the motifs of killing one's desires and dying by divine kiss are fixed topics of philosophical and ethical discourse. Combined, they represent the two poles of spiritual action – of means and ends. On the one side, philosophical apprehension grows with "practicing death"; and on the other, intellectual perfection is fulfilled by a consummate rapture. Shem Tov ibn Falaquera provides repeated examples of the need to subject or control the earthly appetites in order that the rational soul be enlivened. "If you kill [*tamit*] your body in seeking the Truth, you will vivify your soul," he remarks in *Sefer ha-Mevaqqesh*,[24] and in comparable words elsewhere.[25] As a praxis, this is certainly more extreme – even ascetical – advice than one might expect from a philosopher who accepted Aristotle's golden mean to guide human behavior.[26] In another work, Falaquera makes the point more formally: "The mean of the appetitive [soul; i.e., the soul governed by base desires] is that one should abandon bodily pleasures, except for what is necessary."[27] Maimonides was not so severe.

On the other side of the spectrum, there is a reward for ascetical rigor and intellectual development – and that is the possibility of cleaving to the divine intellect. This superior state is figured as a kiss, even as a divine kiss whereby one dies and acquires immortality. Among the first philosophical commentators of the Song of Songs, Moses ibn Tibbon interprets Songs 1:2 ("let him kiss me") as an indication "that the cleaving of the human soul with the Separate Intellect is possible";[28] and Yitzḥaq ibn Sahula makes a similar point.[29] In philosophical tracts, Isaac ibn Laṭif speaks more precisely when he says that the cleaving of the human intellect to the Active Intellect takes "the form of the kiss";[30] and Moses Narboni adopts the commentator's style when he says: "Let Him kiss him with the kisses of His mouth, and let him receive the active intellect in the light of his soul which rises upon her."[31] The femininity of the soul and the masculinity of the divine intellect, combined with the figure of the kiss and the idiom "rises upon her," give this portrayal of an intellectual conjunction a starkly erotic cast. It is a *hieros gamos,* or sacred marriage of sorts, in the most (philosophically) idealized of terms.

Death and Desire in Jewish Spirituality

A combination of the theme of *eros* with spiritual death is noted by Rabbi Baḥye ben Asher in his biblical commentary (on Deuteronomy 34:4) and in his theological dictionary *Kad ha-Qemaḥ*. The entire theme is epitomized near the end of the entry "Love" and provides a concise summary of our preceding discussion.

Now with regard to this high rank of intense love was the Song of Songs established, for it begins: "Let him kiss me with the kisses of his mouth"; and our blessed sages explained [it thus]: "all the writings are holy, but the Song of Songs is the Holy of Holies," for the end of what is sought from humankind is to cleave the intellect to the Holy of Holies [viz., the heavenly attributes], and indeed the very word "kiss" means cleaving. . . . Now our master Moses, of blessed memory, achieved this high rank; for his death was by a kiss. Thus did our blessed sages explain: "'And Moses the servant of the Lord died there in the land of Moab by the mouth of the Lord,' meaning that he died by a kiss." Now the word "kiss" means the cleaving of the lover with the beloved [lit., the subject of intense love with its object]; and by this means the soul separates from this world without any sense of death whatever.[32]

The means to attain the kiss of God varies. For the philosophers, intellectual training provided a curriculum of discipline and a development of the apprehension of the divine realities. But there was also rabbinic tradition and its regimen of piety and control. Its purpose, according to Maimonides, is functional: to guide one away from worldly matters and toward single-minded devotion to God. "Know," he counsels, "that all the practices of the worship, such as reading the *Torah,* prayer, and the performance of the other *commandments,* have only the end of training you to occupy yourself with His commandments,

may He be exalted, rather than with matters pertaining
to this world" (*Guide* III.51). Through the Law, then,
one could begin to imitate David, who said, "I have set
the Lord always before me" (Psalm 16:8), and to fulfill
the advice of the sages: "Do not let God be absent from
your thought" (*b. Shabbat* 149*a*).[33]

But there is a more interior training afforded by the
Law. This has several aspects. To begin with, Maimonides
says, one should attempt to empty the mind of everything
and recite the Shema prayer (Deuteronomy 6:4–9) with
focused intent. This combination of *kenosis* (or self-
emptying) and meditative devotion isolates the mind from
worldly things and sets it on the course of loving God with
all one's heart (mind) and soul and might. It is a practice, he
notes, that must be "carried out correctly" and "practiced
consistently for years." Only then can one begin to take
the second and third steps on this path, which consist of
reflective attention on the Torah and prophetic lections
and on all benedictions – free of distracting thoughts.
These practices also require arduous devotion and must
be practiced consistently. It is only after this discipline
is perfected that one is properly prepared to attend to
"things pertaining to this world" – be they the necessities
of life, the welfare of the body, or fellowship with one's
family – without losing spiritual balance. Nevertheless,
worldly matters of whatever sort must never occupy one's
thoughts while "performing the actions imposed by the
Law." With respect to the commandments, the adept
must render to God single-minded service and separate
meditative praxis from personal and social demands. The
"governance of the solitary" takes priority (in principle
and in practice) over the "governance of the household."

But all this pertains to external, public behaviors.
During more private moments ("when you are alone

with yourself and no one else is there, and while you lie awake in your bed") another praxis is advocated. And that is that the devotee should engage exclusively in the intellectual worship of God. Awakened to the love of God by a philosophical apprehension of the true realities, the worshipper will employ intellectual thought in *constantly* loving Him. Such permanence is the goal of true life and is "[m]ostly . . . . achieved in solitude and isolation."[34] But insofar as the adept isolates his mind from external things, profound attachment to God can be achieved even within the interhuman realm. This is truly the highest stage of meditative practice and overcomes the split between intellectual attention on divine things during worship and occupying one's thoughts with worldly things otherwise. In this state one may outwardly be with people but inwardly wholly turned toward God. This exceptional level of consciousness, of which more will be said later, is the highest rung of philosophical meditation. For Maimonides, nothing better captures this reality than a "poetical parable" in the Song of Songs (5:2): "I sleep, but my heart is awake; the voice of my beloved knocks." In this remarkable reading, a new testimony is given: not the excited fantasy of desire but a numbing of the exterior senses so that the presence of God may be acquired in pure inwardness. In time and with proper devotion the lover may hope for a kiss and thereby exchange this world for the world to come.

In more mystical circles, spiritual death is not deferred to the end of life and does not depend upon halakhic practice per se. To be sure, traditional devotion may be a vaunted exercise, but the onset of the ecstasy is triggered by other effects. These nonhalakhic behaviors may be enthusiastic, unregulated celebrations, or they may be part of a regimen of meditative techniques developed by certain masters and requiring austere training and perseverance. The result may be either a temporary state of mystical dying or physical death in utter bliss. In some cases the adept may even choose between the two while in a state of ecstatic consciousness.

An extraordinary example of sudden death in ecstasy is preserved in the *Sod ha-Shalshelet,* from the end of the thirteenth or the beginning of the fourteenth century.[35] Preceding the key episode, there is a brief discussion of the employment of the cantillation note called *shalshelet* by the Levites and high priest in the ancient Temple. This musical tone was part of a "science of music" known to these holy men and used for various songs and for the pronunciation of the divine Name. These produce a state of exalted "joy" or bliss, which is an influx from the Holy Spirit. But such effects were not limited to sacral virtuosi, for we are immediately told:

Such also was the incident of the two young French girls in the city of the volcano [= Montpellier], in ancient times. They knew how to perform music, and they had a pleasant voice, and they excelled in the science of music. They began to recite [Psalm 45:1]: "To the chief musician upon Shoshannim, for the sons of Korah, Maskil, A Song of Loves." They chanted according to the straight path, and they fused with the higher [entities], and they were so absorbed in song that before they finished half the psalm, God rejoiced at hearing the song from their mouths, as is His way. The tune rose upwards, they achieved union, and their souls ascended to Heaven. See how God rejoices at hearing a tune done correctly, and how much power there is in good music!

We thus have a record of a special musical tradition known to two young girls. They knew the "science of

music" and applied it to Psalm 45. In the process of
their recitation, they became absorbed in their song and,
through it, in the divine realities – so much so that their
souls ascended in union with God, and they expired. The
verb used to express the medial and final state of spiritual
conjunction is *davaq*, a technical term for mystical cleaving; and the expression for spiritual expiration, *pareḥah
nishmatan*, recalls the idiom in *Songs Rabba* describing the
death of the Israelites at the sound of God's command.
Even more crucial for appreciating this testimony is the
fact that the girls were reciting Psalm 45, whose initial line
refers to a "Song of Loves," a *shir yedidot*. This suggests
that the recitation was an ecstatic love song to God, which
was received in joy and reciprocated by the absorption
of the holy souls on high. Stimulating divine bliss, the
girls died in love – conjoined to God.

A more deliberate practice linked to our theme of
eros and *thanatos* occurs in the *Me'irat 'Einayim*, by Rabbi
Isaac of Acre (ca. 1270–1350). This great disciple of
Nahmanides provides a practice based on visualization of
the Tetragrammaton in order to achieve a state of union
with God. The adept is urged to fix attention on God's
Name by placing "the letters of the Unique Name before
his inner eye [lit., the eyes of his intellect and thought]
as if they were written before him on a scroll written in
square script [lit., Ashurite], with each letter of infinite
extent."[36] This is the "secret of binding one's soul Above
and causing one's thought to cleave to the Exalted God"
so as to acquire eternal life in the world to come. This
process is gradual and perfective, for "in proportion
to one's knowledge . . . will be the [degree of] cleaving
of one's thought [on high]; and in proportion to one's
cleaving to Him will be [the seeker's] exaltation and soul
in the world to come – until it [viz., the soul] departs

from his body with a kiss and returns to its source."[37]
The entire passage is reminiscent of Maimonides: in the
relationship between thought and love, in the release of
the soul by a kiss, and in the individual effort to place the
Lord before one's mind always. The significant difference
lies in the means employed, which for Rabbi Isaac is a
technique of inner vision centered on the iconography
of the Name. Through such devoted practice one might
escape evil "happenings" in the here and now and acquire
immortality.[38] Maimonides thought likewise.[39] It may
therefore be supposed that Rabbi Isaac had access to the
Guide and, in particular, those mystical interpretations
of it that were available in Spain through the disciples of
Rabbi Abraham Abulafia.

In other writings, Rabbi Isaac speaks of spiritual
cleaving as a type of absorption by which the soul is
"swallowed" by God.

When the pious *maskil* [intellectual seeker] causes his soul
to ascend so as to cleave in a correct manner [lit., cleaving]
to the divine mystery to which she cleaves, [God] swallows
her. And this is the secret of the verse [in Numbers 4:20],
"but they shall not come in to see when the holy things are
concealed [lit., swallowed],[40] lest they die."[41]

This assimilation of the soul to the divine is clearly an
ultimate mystical state – a death in ecstasy.[42] Much like
the image of a divine kiss, the human soul is absorbed by
God after it achieves a perfected level of cleaving. Two
stages are thus involved: active and passive. At the outset,
the soul strives to connect with God, with greater and
more permanent results. But once this goal is realized,
the soul is swallowed up.

Other passages indicate a transitional step in this mystical process, through the related image of "sinking" into

Death and Desire in Jewish Spirituality

the ocean of divinity. Rabbi Isaac employs this term in the context of discussing the dangers of mystical rapture and seems to distinguish between a viable contemplation of the divine light and a more extreme form which results in "sinking" (*ṭeviʿah*).[43] The repeated cautions to "guard yourself" or "try to see [the Upper Light] and escape [its dangers]" suggest a residual amount of will between the intention to cleave and the loss of willpower in ecstasy. A comparable moment of decision is recorded in an anonymous mystical collection roughly contemporary with Rabbi Isaac. Here another "death scene" is reported, but with an unexpected twist.

Ben Azzai gazed and died, for he looked upon the splendor of the Shekhinah . . . ; and after his cleaving to it he did not want to separate from that sweet splendor, and [so] remained immersed [*ṭavuʿa*] and hidden within it; and his soul was crowned and wreathed by that splendor and radiance which no creature can cleave to and thereafter live, as is written [in Exodus 33:20], "for no person may see Me and live."[44]

This account is based on the famous episode of "Four Who Entered (a) *Pardes*," preserved in several rabbinic versions. It is possible that this pericope was originally merely a hortatory parable about four sages who entered a royal garden[45] – with different results. In several versions we learn that "ben Azzai gazed and was stricken," "ben Zoma gazed and died," "Elisha ben Abuya [or Aḥer] cut the shoots," and "Rabbi Akiba entered safely and departed safely" (lit., in peace).[46] In the account found in the Babylonian Talmud (b. Ḥagiga 14b) the roles of ben Azzai and ben Zoma are switched,[47] so that it is the former who "gazed and died"; and this is the version upon which the foregoing elaboration is based. In addition to

34

the same treatment of ben Azzai, this account presumes that he had a mystical experience – and just this motif is present in the talmudic text. Following the rubric "Four Who Entered (a) *Pardes*" and before the report of their experiences, Rabbi Akiba warned them about a visionary illusion in the upper heavens. This transforms the garden into a mystic realm – a paradise – and the entry into it a mystical flight of the soul.[48] In fact, Akiba is said to have "ascended and descended" in peace.[49]

At first glance it would therefore seem that the Babylonian Talmud's version of the rabbinic episode is a cautionary teaching about the dangers of mystical vision – insofar as it can lead to death, madness, or apostasy unless one is properly trained and focused. But at some early stage various proof texts were added to the pericope to explicate the meaning of the instruction. By citing Songs 1:4 ("Draw me after you . . . ; the king has brought me into his chambers") in connection with Akiba, there is clearly an attempt to state that the true mystic begins with a humble request and is then taken up by God in rapture into the heavenly palaces. Similarly, by means of Proverbs 25:16 ("If you have found honey, eat only what you need, lest you glut yourself and vomit it up") ben Zoma's injury is deemed the result of an intemperate spiritual appetite. The case of Elisha ben Abuya is more complex. The verse cited ("Do not bring your flesh into sin, and do not say before the angel that it is an error"; Ecclesiastes 5:5) also suggests an incautious act during the mystical state (which we know to be an improper assessment of the status of the angel Metatron in heaven); and such behavior may rightly be another case of pride before a fall.[50]

This brings us to ben Azzai, whose death is followed by the remark: "Precious in the eyes of the Lord is the death of His righteous ones" (Psalm 116:15). This is clearly a positive evaluation; and one may conclude that, in contrast to Rabbi Akiba, who experienced mystical bliss and returned to the world, ben Azzai died in rapture, and that this death pleased the Lord.[51] The medieval epitome of this event cited above follows this understanding, with the added information that between the initial cleaving and ultimate sinking ben Azzai decided not "to separate from that sweet splendor" but to remain immersed in a flood of supernal light. He thus died in a state of the sweetest bliss.

A further transformation of ben Azzai into a medieval mystic occurs in the mystical Torah commentary of Rabbi Menaḥem Recanati (late thirteenth to early fourteenth century). Citing the rabbinic tradition in which Rabbi Akiba came upon ben Azzai in trance and thought him to be dealing with the supernal secrets of the Heavenly Chariot (*Songs Rabba* 1.10.ii), Recanati interprets ben Azzai's response ("I was sitting and reciting and the words [*devarim*] descended . . . before me") as referring to a technique of visualization. "When he had caused his soul to cleave to the Upper Soul, the awesome words [*devarim*] were engraved in his mind and he would draw them [before his inner eye].[52] As distinct from Rabbi Isaac's aforementioned technique of cleaving to a visual icon of the divine Name, we now see that the visualization of "awesome *devarim*" is induced by the state of conjunction with the supernal soul – for through the divine efflux thus brought forth "the elements expand and increase" joyfully in his consciousness. A slightly different sequence seems to be reported for the ancient "pious and practical ones." Recanati says that when engaged in "supernal mysteries" these mystics began by visualizing things; and then, when they caused their souls to cleave to the higher realms, these "things" began "expanding" and

Death and Desire in Jewish Spirituality

"appearing of themselves" from the source of thought. [53] It may be that there is no real difference between the two methods, in which case ben Azzai also began with an imaginative visualization based on a (weak) conjunction with divine realities; and as his cleaving increased, so were the shapes of the representation successively enlarged. In any case, the repeated reference to "the things increasing and expanding" is undoubtedly drawn from Rabbi Azriel of Gerona's commentary. [54]

At this point, Recanati goes on to say that it may happen that the utter "joy" or pleasure of this meditative state will induce in the adept "a mighty and overwhelming cry [bekhiyah], and his spirit and soul will desire to separate from his body." This is an exalted moment, different from the technique of crying in order to induce a mystical experience [55] and from the instances of weeping following such ecstasy. [56] It is a state between initial rapture and uttermost expiration, reminiscent of the case of ben Azzai, who decided at such a point to remain in supernal transport and die. Indeed, in the present instance the decisive moment is a last gasp of this-worldly consciousness and is expressed as a cry of absolute longing for permanent union with God. Recanati aptly comments here that "this [separation of the soul from the body] is death by [the] kiss [of God]."

To clarify his point, Recanati adduces a tradition from the *Zohar* (III. 144a-b) which speaks of the ecstatic death of Rabbi Yose, Rabbi Hizkiyah, and Rabbi Yeisa upon receiving an astonishing mythical-theosophical revelation about the primordial emanation. As the remaining comrades watched the holy angels transporting their friends off in a canopy, [57] they were greatly distraught by the possibility that they too had sinned and would be punished for revealing esoteric knowledge. They were assuaged by a heavenly reply confirming their blessed

Death and Desire in Jewish Spirituality

"portion" and imparting the knowledge that the souls of their comrades cleaved to the divine at the very moment of death. [58] The *Zohar* adds that the "souls [of the three comrades] departed with a kiss" and were bound to the ascending canopy. And "why did [just] these die? Because on an earlier occasion they had entered and not emerged; [whereas] all the others 'had entered and emerged.'" The last clearly alludes to the mystical experience of Rabbi Akiba, who entered the heavenly realms and returned "in peace." [59] By contrast, the ecstatic death of the three comrades recalls ben Azzai. Like them, he died in rapture.

One final image deserves comment. It occurs in the *Zohar* (II.124*b*), in the course of a comment on Songs 1:2. As in the commentary of ibn Sahula, here a reference to individual death by divine kiss is preceded by a hypostatic reading of the verse. It is thus not the earthly beloved who calls to her male lover but the supernal Female (called "Community of Israel") in quest of conjunction with her heavenly Spouse (Jacob-Israel). In the process, the older midrashic reading is transformed. No longer grounded in national history, the locus of the song becomes metahistorical. [60] Accordingly, the desire for a kiss is nothing less than a yearning for union *within* the divine realm. But now the *Zohar* raises a question. Why does the text read "let him kiss me" and not "let him love me" – as might be expected? And the answer is that the word "kisses" indicates "the cleaving of spirit to spirit"; for just as kisses derive from the mouth, which is "the source and outlet of spirit," so are heavenly kisses a permanent bonding of Spirit to Spirit. In similar vein, the *Zohar* concludes that "one whose soul departs with a [divine] kiss cleaves to another spirit – one that is inseparable from it." A perfected death thus replicates supernal conjunctions, insofar as the spiritual cleaving of the female (human) soul to the divine at death resembles the perfect conjunction of spirits in the heavenly realm. And according to zoharic theosophy, such a human act also induces the intradivine union. In this way, the death of the saints repairs the cosmos itself.

The zoharic tradition of ecstatic death by divine kiss is not affected by philosophical notions or vocabulary, which distinguishes it from the Maimonidean reworking of the talmudic tradition, as well as from the mystical adaption of Maimonides by Abraham Abulafia (1240–ca. 1291) and his disciples. This latter development is particularly interesting for the way it senses mystical potential in the "affective intellectualism" of the *Guide* and for its development of technical practices wholly distinct from the halakhic discipline of the *Mishneh Torah*. Certainly Maimonides' own references to private meditation techniques and his ideal of self-redemption through impassioned attachment (cleaving) to God inspired Abulafia. Equally influential was the soul-body dualism and the necessity to control the passions in order that the soul may bond with God forever.

As noted earlier, Maimonides spoke of a progressive development of the soul toward such spiritual release: "[I]n the measure that the faculties of the body are weakened . . . the intellect is strengthened, . . . its apprehension is purified, and it rejoices in what it apprehends . . . – until the soul is separated from the body . . . in this state of pleasure" (*Guide* III. 51). Abulafia gives a distinctly mystical explication to this passage in *Sefer Ḥayyei ha-'Olam ha-Ba'*:

The more the divine [intellective] influx is strengthened within you, the more your external and internal organs will weaken, and your body will begin to tremble very greatly, until you think that you are about to die; for your soul becomes separated from your body due to the great joy in retaining and knowing what you have known.[61]

As against Maimonides' discussion, where the foregoing passage occurs as part of an ideal of intellectual apprehension of God by means of meditative techniques preparatory to the goal of weakening the senses and death by divine kiss, Abulafia's remark follows an instruction concerning the meditational permutations of letters, which produce a state of ecstatic "heat" and elicit an influx of "knowledge . . . not derived from intellectual analysis." The flood of the divine influx (*shefaʿ*) is then described in the above citation, along with the sensation of death in rapture. The adept is then told "to choose life over death" at this moment (viz., to "let go" of mortal attachments) for the sake of the resurrection of his soul (from physical incarnation). That this technique of "dying" is not a final act (as in Maimonides) is evidenced by Abulafia's remark that the disciple should master this practice of "choosing life," and then he will be ready for a higher method. It is only in connection with mortal death while pronouncing the divine Name that the master speaks of death by divine kiss.[62]

Drawing on old rabbinic tradition, a disciple of Abulafia refers to a willed spiritual death through a juxtaposition of citations reminiscent of Isaac Israeli:

[F]or in truth, ʾif a man lives it, that man will live; as the philosophers say: "If you wish to live by nature, die voluntarily and live by nature; and if you wish to die by nature, live voluntarily and die by nature." And this is clear to a man who has been granted by God knowledge and understanding and intellect; blessed be He who has graced us with knowledge. And our sages said likewise, in their saying: "What shall man do to live? He shall die. And what shall man do to die? He shall live."[63]

Abulafia himself cites this talmudic saying from *b. Tamid* 32*a* ("What shall man do . . . ?") in a revelation of a mystical "secret" about true life and goes on to say that this theme is also hinted at in Numbers 19:14, "If a man dies in his tent."[64] This passage had long been a set piece on the asceticism of Torah study, based on an interpretation by Resh Lakish ("The words of Torah are realized only through one who kills himself over them"; *b. Giṭṭin* 57*b*). Abulafia cites this tradition and adds that "the Rabbi [Maimonides] said in *Sefer ha-Mada'* . . . that the Torah is realized only by one who kills himself in the tents of wisdom."[65] For Maimonides this "wisdom" is the inner philosophical sense of the Torah, and its end is a perfected apprehension resulting in spiritual death. Abulafia sought the Active Intellect through theurgical meditations and yearned to die in the rapture of its bountiful flow.

The Abulafian technique of physical isolation and rhythmic recitations of holy letters was carried on by his disciples. A remarkable manual in this tradition, outlining a whole regimen of spiritual ascent, is preserved in the *Sullam ha-'Aliyah* of Rabbi Judah Albuṭini (Jerusalem; early sixteenth century).[66] Indeed the important tenth chapter contains an "explanation of the ways of meditation, and cleaving, and the proper preparations for the adept to follow in order to attain the goal of [his mental] intention – that he conjoin his soul with the Active Intellect and receive the Holy Spirit [of prophecy]." The preparations themselves include control of the physical passions (that "the intellect escape the prison of animal instincts"), acts of bodily purification, correction of moral attributes, equanimity of the spirit, and single-minded concentration on the divine intelligibilia.[67] Thus, "*ascetical withdrawal* leads to *purification* of the [natural] instincts and *cleanliness* of the [moral] attributes; equanimity leads to the concentration [or isolation] of the [higher] soul; and concentration leads to *the Holy Spirit*, which leads to prophecy – which is the highest level." Clearly this ladder of ascent reworks the ancient program of piety (*ḥasidut*) taught by Rabbi Pinḥas ben Yair, who said: "caution leads to *cleanliness*, cleanliness leads to *purity*, purity leads to holiness, holiness leads to humility, humility leads to fear of sin, fear of sin leads to piety, piety leads to the *Holy Spirit*, the Holy Spirit leads to the resurrection of the dead, [and] the resurrection of the dead leads to Elijah, may he be remembered for good."[68] The notable difference is Albuṭini's substitution of contemporary Sufic-Stoic ideals (of equanimity and concentration) for the ethical-saintly virtues of the ancient sage, and his replacement of the hope in physical resurrection and national eschatology with the goal of spiritual restoration and redemption of the individual soul.

The practical means of achieving personal salvation by becoming united with the Active Intellect is then described. Various preparations of site and sense are advised, along with creating mental images and reciting divine Names. As the intellect of the adept separates from this-worldly constraints and becomes "active," "he will collapse to the ground like a dead man" and receive an influx of the divine that will anoint him with heavenly grace – for he has escaped into the divine realm.

And then his soul is simplified and rejuvenated through conjunction with the root of the Source from which it was hewn. And it may happen that his soul will completely separate [from his body] during this period of simplification and remain dead; and such a death is exalted and somewhat like death by [divine] kiss. And in this way did the soul of ben Azzai [who "looked and died"] separate; for his soul rejoiced upon seeing the Source from which it was hewn and desired to cleave to it and remain there and not return to the body. And regarding his death it is said, "Precious in the eyes of the Lord is the death of His righteous ones."

The text continues with the remark that mystics engaged in this "practice" can prevent such an occurrence if, while still in the human realm (having fallen comatose but not yet overwhelmed by the influx), they swear against it. Then they may return alive to the world and even repeat this technique of "choosing life" until they become experts.[69] This allusion to Abulafia's *Sefer Ḥayyei ha-'Olam ha-Ba'* is supplemented by two explicit references to that work and its method of manipulating holy Names.

The Abulafian tradition of meditative ecstasy, culminating in prophecy, also appears in the writings of the sixteenth-century Kabbalist Rabbi Ḥayyim Viṭal, the great disciple of Rabbi Isaac Luria of Safed. Of particular interest is the tract called *Sha'arei Qedushah*. Here he describes the proper preparations for beginning the meditative processes that induce the divine influx. Various sequences are spelled out. These include repentance, moral attributes, humility, and equanimity (III.4); and repentance, caution, moral attributes, ascetical withdrawal, (physical) purity, concentration, and reception of the Holy Spirit (III.7). Save for the initial element, the process resembles that found in Albuṭini. Significantly, part IV opens with a citation of the stages of moral-spiritual development taught by Pinḥas ben Yair, followed by a whole cluster of citations from later authors.[70] These constitute a virtual chain of authorities on the subject and indicate the great value placed on a genealogy of masters. All of the authors we have considered (and many more) figure here, including Abraham Abulafia, Isaac of Acre, and Menaḥem Recanati (IV. 1–2). A chart of holy Names used to induce ecstasy follows (IV. 3): the awesome mantra of the Seventy-two Names of God, in all their mysterious vocables. It is followed by another tradition for generating the divine influx, about which the author remarks: "In my humble opinion this is what is written in the *Sefer Ḥayyei ha-'Olam ha-Ba'*, but it is much abbreviated [there]." The quote actually comes from Abulafia's *Sefer ha-Ḥeshek*.

In Part III, chapter 8 (the final part before the holy Names are disclosed), Viṭal elaborates on the inner state of the mystic during his preparation for receiving the Holy Spirit. It is part of a sequence of purifications, and recalls the teachings of Abulafia and Albuṭini. Here we encounter the theme of death in rapture.

The Fifth [purification] is this: When [the adept] shall prepare himself to receive the Holy Spirit, after all the good qualities have been thoroughly internalized, he should enter a solitary dwelling with purity and holiness – a place where the sounds of humans or the chirping of birds cannot disturb him. The time after midnight is the most suitable for such matters. [Then] let him shut his eyes and divest his thought from all matters pertaining to this world, *as if his soul departed from him, as from a dead man, who feels nothing.* After this he should strive with a great effort to think of the upper worlds and cleave there to the root of his soul and to the supernal lights. *And let him imagine himself as if his soul departed and ascended on high.* And let him make a configuration of the higher worlds as if he were standing in them. And if he achieved any unification, let him meditate on it and thereby draw light and [the divine] influx through all the worlds.

Death and Desire in Jewish Spirituality

Of particular note is the role accorded the imagination in this praxis. Two acts are mentioned. The first comes after the mystic is told to block out the world and its sensations – "as if" (*ke'ilu*) he were dead. This done, he should first "imagine" himself "as if" dead and his soul in supernal ascent. Monitoring his transport, the adept should then draw mental images of the divine worlds "as if" he stood therein. The hypothetical construction is intriguing. Presumably the dual sense of having a body in this world and a soul in another produces a bifurcated consciousness – and this is captured by the phrase "as if." Death and ecstasy are thus experienced from within but viewed from without. This results in screen images of the sensate soul, while in the very process of its simplification.[71]

A third contemporary of Albuṭini and Viṭal, Rabbi Joseph Karo of Safed, gave exegetical expression to this sense of death when the soul is freed of physical constraints and begins (with increasing intensity) to cleave to the divine. Indeed, he does not focus on the techniques of ecstasy but on their spiritual end when he reports this advice from his celestial mentor:

Let your soul cleave to your Creator, and thus death will be for you a rest. This is the true meaning of what our sages said: "He who wants to live should die." . . . and by this path [of mortification] it is like killing oneself. Thereby one truly revives one's soul, and separation from this world will be felt as a profound rest by cleaving to the Creator. For if the soul adhered to the Creator even while imprisoned in this vile body, how much more will it cleave to the Creator and be illumined by the light of life once it has separated itself from matter?[72]

The passage stresses death as the perfect realization of cleaving to God and invokes an epitome from *b. Tamid*

45

32*a* for this purpose. Such a notion is an old theme, as we have seen, with roots in Maimonides. But the Kabbalist gives the topos a mystical twist by focusing on the death and revival of the soul in the here and now. Note that he says that one who "truly revives" his soul (lit., causes it to live) will experience its separation from worldliness as a kind of rest. He thus implies a state of mystical trance while in the world, which is reminiscent of Maimonides' interpretation of Songs 5:2 ("I am asleep, but my heart is awake"). This exalted state is a rest from the prison of the "vile body." Indeed it is a kind of death-in-life, if we can assume that Karo was alluding to Job 3:13. In that passage, Job desires release from the torment of time and yearns for death and the solace of the grave, where "I would sleep and find rest." Karo has transfigured that desire.

The chastening of bodily needs, as what one does to "kill" oneself ('*atzmo*), is repeatedly stressed by Karo. It is a spiritual program of uncompromising intensity that often uses sacrificial images to express the consummation of desire.[73] This topos recurs in the early generations of Hasidism as well, despite the general trend to neutralize the ascetical practices of earlier moralists. Particularly striking, therefore, is the following private prayer attributed to the Ba'al Shem Tov:

Behold, I desire to kill [viz., mortify] myself in order to serve the Name, be He blessed, in truth and with a whole heart, in love and fear, that I acknowledge His Unity fully. Therefore, I desire to kill myself – even to sacrifice myself as an oblation before Him.[74]

In this passage the Ba'al Shem articulates his desire for continuous self-sacrifice before God, a sacrifice of the self, or ego; for all the while one's lower self is palpable,

Death and Desire in Jewish Spirituality

it creates a duality, so to speak, in the divine unity. Only utter self-negation can lead to a magnification of God's Name; that is to say, true worship can occur only with a sacrifice or killing (*le-hamit*) of one's natural "self" (called here *'atzmiy*). With this, one can perceive a bold reinterpretation of the talmudic teaching of the scholars of the south, who, almost two millennia earlier, answered the query, "What should one do to live?" with the reply, *yamit 'et 'atzmo,* "Let him kill himself."

The ideal of utter self-negation, of a *kenosis* of sorts, continues among subsequent masters, like the Maggid of Mezeritzch and Rabbi Levi Yitzhak of Berdichev (who went to study with the Maggid in 1766). Indicative is the following interpretation of *b. Tamid* 32a, reported by Rabbi Ya'akov Yitzhak ha-Levi of Lublin in the name of Rabbi Levi Yitzhak, then of Pinsk:

He said: "Whoever wants to live should kill himself." I heard [the following] from the Rabbi of Pinsk, may he live, who interpreted [thus]: Whoever wants to live should disregard his bodily concerns and cause his thought to cleave to the Creator, blessed be He. And [by] this [means], "he shall kill himself"; [that is] he shall withdraw from himself – however, he is nevertheless alive, since he cleaves to the Life [force] of [all] life. . . . Whoever is impoverished by his cleaving to the Creator, blessed be He, is certainly considered . . . as dead and released from [real] death, because "he lives in them" [viz., the commandments; Leviticus 18:5].[75]

The paradoxes of life and death suffuse this exegetical account of mystical experience. It follows a pattern seen earlier, though with the specific caveat that the act of cleaving to God, which causes the soul to depart the body, is a killing of oneself, an act of self-annihilation. This

47

death act is nonetheless a resurrection to true life, since the soul is conjoined to the source of life. But though the soul has fully departed and therefore has no need of being released at physical death, the body remains in this world. The adept thus exists in a spiritual trance or "sleep" and remains alive as an existent being through the commandments. Were he to cease performing these duties, which draw their sustenance from the "Life [force] of [all] life," mortal death would follow. The realized mystic therefore cannot become utterly quiescent.[76]

Except in the depths of prayer. This was a realm inhabited by the Maggid of Mezeritzch, the great disciple of the Ba'al Shem and teacher of Levi Yitzhak. From the secrets of contemplative prayer he revealed the following teaching.[77] He begins with a string of citations:

"Rabba bar bar Hana said to me: I have seen the 'dead of the desert' [cf. Numbers 14:29, 32], and they were in a state of exhilaration [lit., upon their backs], etc." [b. Baba Bathra 73b]. This matter is like that mentioned in the Talmud [Gemara]: "Whoever wants to live should kill himself" [b. Tamid 32a]; and also, "The Torah is realized only by one who kills himself for it" [b. Gittin 57b], as is written, "This is the Torah: one who dies in a tent" [Numbers 19:14]. Now one must comprehend the [true] meaning of death here.

To explain this, Rabbi Dov Ber (the Maggid) begins with an analogy of a student who, after some difficulty, penetrates the teachings of his master and becomes so absorbed that he cannot respond to one who calls him. Such a profound absorption, says the Maggid, "is almost like death or sleep, which is one-sixtieth of death." In a similar way does silent thought transcend speech; for when thought leaves the limitations of language, it enters into the world of Thought (a higher realm in the Kabbala) and the mind is enlarged. A yet higher and more profound example of this phenomenon occurs in the course of verbal prayer when the limitations of words and corporeal reality are temporarily transcended, and there is an enlargement of consciousness in a state of silent exhilaration. "And this," the Maggid concludes, "[is the true sense of] 'I have seen the dead of the desert' [*meytei midbar*]; that is, whoever kills himself [viz., annihilates (*meymit*) his selfhood (*'atzmo*)] in the words [*dibburei*] of prayer, as explained above. [And with regard to the phrase] 'and they were in a state of exhilaration,' this means [that they were enraptured] because they utterly emptied their minds, as in sleep, as explained above."

In this profound discourse, the Maggid puns on the talmudic reference to the dead of the desert (*midbar*), who were in a state of exhilaration, and considers it an allegory for those who would abandon their everyday speech (*midibbur*) in order to achieve the rapture of silent communication with God. Such a spiritual death in prayer overcomes self-centeredness. It is a killing or annihilation of one's self (*'atzmo*) in order to realize divine reality. All attachments to speech and its worldly echoes must be transcended. That is what one must do in order to live.

Let me conclude with a modern meditation on the transcendence of speech found in the poem "Ha-Bereikhah" (The Pool), by Ḥayyim Naḥman Bialik.[78] Here the poet reveals his great desire to receive once again – "if for one brief moment" – the "first sweetness" of his childhood. He knows that "the splendid vision is never granted twice"; but he nevertheless waits like a tempered harp for that angelic gift of a world pure and unviolated, "with God's wonder on my face." And then it happens,

Death and Desire in Jewish Spirituality

by the silent pool in a wood "dripping shadow and light."
Filled with its "sacred desires my heart trembles, expires,
and dies" (*ube-ma'avayei qodsho libbi yakhil, yikhleh, yigva'*),
and "the voice of the hiding God" breaks the silence and
asks, "Where are you?" The poet has died to his former
self and receives the revelation of God. And God teaches
him purely, in the "silent immanent language," in the
"shades of hues" of the world, and in the "sea's wrath"
and "the roar of light." Looking into the pool, the poet
beholds the eye of the Forest Prince: "great in mysteries.
And in patient, profound meditation."

Thus it was as foretold long ago: "If you wish to
live, then die." To be reborn with a heavenly vision
one must first transcend worldly wisdom and all things
selfish. Bialik thus echoes a long Jewish tradition which
considered the perfected love of God a return to the realm
of paradise. One must die somehow, in some measure, in
order to pass the fiery sword that guards the gates of Eden,
the eternal realm of God. For the poet, this supernatural
reality is the heart of nature.

2

"For Your sake we are killed all day long"

The Sanctification of God in Love

In the preceding chapter we had occasion to consider aspects of death and desire in Jewish spirituality as they pertain to the spiritual quest. A central metaphor of that quest is the "kiss of God," when the perfected human soul dies in a supernatural rapture. As remarked, the talmudic source for this "death by divine kiss" implies a more natural death – though one graced by God. Such a death is a reward for righteousness in the classical rabbinic sense: a painless release from the bonds of mortality. One striking piece of exegesis makes the point plain. Commenting on Psalm 68:21, "God, the Lord, provides an escape from death [*la-mavet totza'ot*]," the sages taught that "903 species of death were created in this world" on the basis of the numerical equivalent of the word *totza'ot* and that "the easiest of them is [death by] the kiss" (*b. Berakhot* 8a). "Some say" that such a death "is like drawing a hair out of milk."

There is yet another type of death by divine kiss. This one marks the wholly unnatural passing of the martyrs who die for the sanctification of the divine Name. Here the kiss signals a blissful attachment to the divine, through

The Sanctification of God in Love

which the faithful overcome the pains of torturous
death. A striking instance of such transcendence is preserved by an interpretation of the statement "One who
obeys the Command [*mitzvah,* of the divine King] will
not experience evil" (Ecclesiastes 8:5) by Rabbi Moshe
Galante, in his sixteenth-century work *Kohelet Ya'aqov*.[1]
Reflecting on the tortures endured by Jews, he said: "In
my opinion, the sense [of this verse] is similar to what is
adduced by the Tosafists . . . following a tradition of
the sages [of France]: 'Those who are burnt and killed
for the sanctification of His Name do not experience this
torment but die [painlessly] by the [divine] kiss.'" If this
is not hyperbole, what is involved?

Rabbinic formulations of this matter, cast as program-
matic counsel, were transmitted for centuries during the
Middle Ages, in both the Franco-German and Spanish
communities. A particularly powerful expression is cited
in the *Tashbetz* of Rabbi Shimshon ben Zadok, in the
name of Rabbi Meir of Rothenberg (1215–95): "When a
person determines in his mind [*gomer be-da'ato*] to sanctify
the Name and devote himself to the sanctification of the
Name, nothing done to him – whether stoning, burning,
burial alive, or hanging – pains him at all. . . . And know
indeed that this is so!"[2] Rabbi Meir knew whereof he
spoke. Drawing on living memory, he goes on to report
the fortitude of the saints who suffered martyrdom in
stoical silence during the Crusades. He concludes with
the additional testimony of those who say, "Insofar
as one recites the Unique Name at the onset [of the
torture] he is assured of enduring the test [of faith]."
Here too one hears an echo of historical events, when
the recitation of the holy Name served some martyrs
at the time of their great trial. As a magical recitation,
this praxis contrasts with the more meditative procedure

The Sanctification of God in Love

performed before the beginning of torture adduced by Rabbi Meir.[3]

A combination of these techniques and other matters bearing on martyrs' love of God is found in a discourse by Rabbi Abraham ben Eliezer Halevi, a Spanish Kabbalist who made his way to Jerusalem after the Expulsion of 1492.[4] It is a tremendous testimonial from the time of the Inquisition to the attempt of Jewish leaders to exhort their communities to remain steadfast before the threats and torments besetting them. The document, called *Megillat Amraphel,* begins with the rabbinic dictum cited earlier and adds a striking practice associated with it.

This is a tradition among the sages: If someone determines in his heart [*gomer be-libbo*] to sacrifice himself for the honor of His great Name – come what will and transpire what may – such a man will not feel the pain of wounds, which torment only those who have not determined [*gameru*] this with all their hearts [*bekhol libbam*]. Now if one lead such a person forth, in order to subject him to the pain and torment of terrible torture (as it came to pass with the holy martyrs, . . . the sons of Hannah, the martyr . . .), and if, at that hour, such a one focuses on the great and awesome Name between his eyes and determines in his heart [*ve-yigmor be-libbo*] to sanctify Him, and [if] he sees the Holy One of Israel, and [if] he can focus [*yadbiq;* lit., "conjoin"] his entire mind and thought on Him, so that the Name [becomes] a blazing fire, and the letters [thereof] shine and extend over the entire world, or if he is able to make the letters grow to the extent of his power: then he can rest assured in his heart that he will resist temptation. His heart is firm, secure in the Lord. He will not feel the pain of wounds and torture, nor tremble with the fear of death. And though this matter seem farfetched to human reason, it has already been experienced and is a tradition of the sages and martyrs and upright of heart.

The Sanctification of God in Love

This is the first part of Rabbi Abraham's discourse. It is centered on a series of meditative and magical practices which ensure spiritual resistance against the fear of a painful death. Indeed, we do not simply have either mental conviction or theurgical technique – but their dramatic combination. Thus, following a statement of determination without reservation (the verb *gomer* connotes a "complete" and total "resolution"), a number of procedures are mentioned, though without specifying the actual methods. First and foremost, the person must visualize the Tetragrammaton in his inner eye at the time of his torment, and then and there resolve to die a martyr. The mental determination is thus joined to a projection of the holy letters before the third eye. If this step is properly accomplished and a vision of God results, the individual must then focus totally on this reality – in fact, must cleave or conjoin his mind to it – so that the divine Name is transfigured and cosmicized in his mind. Should all this come to pass, says Rabbi Abraham, the martyr can be assured of steadfastness to the end as well as the absence of physical pain.

The situations vary, but there is a striking similarity between this procedure and the mystical practice of Rabbi Isaac of Acre discussed in the previous chapter.[5] It will be recalled that this adept taught the visualization of the divine Name, its magnification in the inner eye, the cleaving of the mind to this reality, and the assurance that constancy in such meditation protected the individual from evil happenstance. Presumably this thirteenth-century Spanish mystical tradition reached Rabbi Abraham, along with the more mental technique noted by Rabbi Meir of Rothenberg, who was Rabbi Isaac's contemporary in the Rhineland.[6] In any event, Rabbi Abraham offers this method as a safeguard from physical fear. Against the

The Sanctification of God in Love

blandishments that the tormenters may offer for apostasy, the martyr should shout: "What do you want from me? I am a Jew! I shall live a Jew and die a Jew! A Jew! A Jew! A Jew!" This threefold climax smacks of an incantation of sorts – all the more suggestive since the Hebrew word for Jew (YHWDY) can, with slight orthographic change, yield the holy Tetragrammaton (YHWH)! So armed, the martyr may prevail.

The conclusion of the *Megillat Amraphel* focuses on the transcendental deliverance of the soul of the martyr who wholeheartedly determines to sanctify the divine Name. This hope and expectation of heavenly bliss under the healing wings of God is an old martyrological theme, already marked in the records of the Rhineland saints from 1096.[7] It was a strong inducement to their superhuman acts. A similar hope is evident in the sermon of Rabbi Abraham ben Eliezer Halevi to his Spanish brethren four centuries later. The whole, poignant conclusion of the text deserves to be heard. In all the Jewish literature of suffering there is, I think, nothing quite like it. The preacher says:

It would seem that it is with respect to the soul of the martyr who devotes his soul to God – who persists in love of Him, dies in the midst of the wicked, and gives his body to the pyre – that [Solomon] the sage said: "Who is this that comes up from the wilderness, pining [*mitrapeqet*] for her beloved?" [Songs 8:5]. For God's word is clear: she is shattered [*mitrapeqet*][8] and falls limb for limb [and] piece for piece [for the sake of her Beloved]. And the righteous who dwell in the innermost reaches of the King's [heavenly] palace, where joy has her habitation, say of the soul of this martyr: "Who is this that comes up from the lower world, which is like a wilderness where there is nothing but serpents and adders, scorpions and thirst? For the love of her Beloved her body falls to pieces [*peraqim peraqim*] in the terrible trials wreaked upon it. They sear her flesh with tongs heated to a white glow and hack it to pieces with the sword." But God, the Lord of peace, for love of whom she suffers all this, looks down from His [heavenly] dwelling and says of the righteous [martyr] whose soul is ascending to Him: "Behold, you are pure and upright! [Therefore] this day have I born you [anew] and 'awakened you under the apple tree' in the orchard of paradise.⁹ And your holy [martyred] soul is purified before your Mother [lit., she who bore you], the Throne of My Glory, whence it was hewn and formed. For where the Throne is, the Mother of all souls, 'there your mother was in travail with you, there she was in travail and bore you' [Songs 8:5]."

Then the righteous [martyr] answers his Creator: "'Set me as a seal upon Your heart, as a seal upon Your arm' [Songs 8:6], and do not forget me for eternity. Remember the love with which I have loved You, for even if they kill me for love of You, I shall not feel it, 'for love is as strong as death' [Songs 8:6]. Indeed, even if they buried me alive this would be as nought to me, for 'my zeal is as fierce as the grave' – my zeal for the honor of Your Name. And even if they burn me and cast me into the fiery furnace, this too is nothing compared to my love of You, for my love of You is a wonder wrought upon me and burns within me like flaming torches, 'the flashes thereof are flashes of fire, a very flame of the Lord' [Songs 8:6]. How, then, could my soul suffer from that little fire when the mighty flame of love for You burns mightily within me? And 'great' tortures and horrors, which are like 'water,' 'cannot quench the' flame of my 'love' [Songs 8:7]. And though torment come as a 'flood' [Songs 8:7], the spirit of the Lord inspires me to devote myself to You. I am not speaking of my property or wealth, for wealth is less than nothing, and if anyone should boast that he gave 'all the substance of his house for love,' those who are perfected, those who come before God, 'would surely scorn him' [Songs 8:7] – for this is without value to those who hold the treasures of the world in contempt." But there is something that one may truly boast of – that he devote his body to the pyre and all the other terrible tortures I spoke about. For such a one will God deem true and place him as a seal upon His right arm, [indeed] affix him like a seal on His heart. His soul shall shine in God's light, and there is no [human] eye that has seen the bliss that awaits it.

As is clear, in this part of the document Rabbi Abraham ben Eliezer Halevi has constructed a series of dialogues based upon an exegetical reworking of the Song of Songs (8:5–7). In fact he regards Solomon's song as a translucent allegory of the martyred soul rising purified to paradise. It is the righteous (and martyred) souls in heaven that speak first (v. 5a), saying, "Who is this that comes up?" For what they in fact see is not the human lover emerging from the steppe but the transfigured soul – cleansed of earthly dross and refined in the fire of faith – ascending to the Throne of Glory. God then looks down from the heights and welcomes the restored and resurrected soul to its heavenly womb. The invitation is based on a figurative reading of the next half-line (v. 5b). There then follows a moving response by the lover (the soul) to the Beloved. It begins with a request that she be set upon God's own arm, so to speak, as a seal that signifies her eternal repose with God (v. 6a) and continues with an account of her fiery passion, beyond compare, before the auto-da-fé. The pangs of death were as nought before the force of her love of God, refining the mettle of her spirit and inuring it to pain (v. 6a–b). This recalls the matter of physical transcendence with which Rabbi Abraham begins and ends his discourse. Perhaps there is some hint here of the inner heat with which mystics are ecstatically enflamed and which deadens the earthly senses. Or perhaps this too is merely a figure emerging from a verse read in light of torture by burning at the stake. At all events, the fire of faith is unquenchable and transcends all blandishments for mortal gain (v. 7). Given Rabbi Abraham's initial division of the prologue into an account of how to overcome physical pain *and* earthly benefit, one may suspect that the concluding contempt of the purified soul for power and wealth fits into this schema. Transfigured, the soul achieves a preternatural bliss: affixed to the body of God and illumined by a transcendental radiance.

In composing this midrashic exhortation, Rabbi Abraham ben Eliezer Halevi has written a theological dialogue for the ages in which one can only glimpse, but scarcely comprehend in all its shattering depth, the absolute love of God that is expressed. The *Megillat Amraphel* not only transforms the national-historical reading of Songs 8:5–7 of the Midrash but also moves on a different plane from the individual-philosophical reading of these verses in the writings of Joseph ibn Aknin or Moses ibn Tibbon. This document is marked both by an allegorical interpretation of the lover as the individual human soul *and* by starkly historical references to the emotional and physical brutalities wrought upon Jews during the Inquisition. Truth to tell, the preacher did not weave this texture from whole cloth but embellished or respun ancient figures on the loom of his genius and experience. Thus, it has been suggested that he drew upon the thirteenth-century mystical *Midrash ha-Ne'elam* (*Zohar* I. 125b), where there are also a dialogical question posed to the ascending soul and the idea that the Mother of souls is the heavenly Throne (based on Songs 8:5 and 6:9, respectively).[10] But this similarity leaves aside the dominant theme of suffering in the homily, and I would therefore propose that Rabbi Abraham's real inspiration was the (thirteenth-century) commentary on

The Sanctification of God in Love

the Song by Rabbi Yitzḥaq ibn Sahula.[11] The following points seem decisive:

1. Rabbi Abraham cites Songs 8:5, which refers to the lover pining (*mitrapeqet*) for her beloved, but then goes on to use this word in the context of physical destruction. That he implies a play with *mitpareqet*, "shattered," is confirmed by the subsequent reference to the hewing of the martyr's body "piece by piece," *peraqim peraqim*. Similarly, ibn Sahula cited Songs 8:5 and adduces Israel's historical sufferings, saying: "She pines for her beloved, and the portions [*pirqei*] of her limbs are broken among the nations."

2. Rabbi Abraham compares the lower world to a wasteland, "where there is nothing but serpents and adders, scorpions and thirst." On 8:5, ibn Sahula compares the exile to just these elements (minus thirst). What is more, both sources speak of the soul ascending to a paradise likened to an apple orchard where the righteous dwell.

3. Referring to the "seal" on God's arm in Songs 8:6, both sources regard the lover as speaking to God and requesting thereby a sign of eternal repose as a reward for martyrdom. Moreover, just as Rabbi Abraham used the comparison of love to death ("for love is as strong as death") to indicate the capacity of the saint's love to deaden the pains of death, ibn Sahula speaks of the "awesome love" for the Beloved that "kills physical sensations."

4. And finally, referring to the unquenchable flame of love in Songs 8:7 Rabbi Abraham refers to the inner flame of the martyr. Ibn Sahula also speaks here of the flame that burns in the soul of the lover of God. For both men the love of God is a "wondrous" grace.[12]

More could be said, but the foregoing may suffice to show the indebtedness of Rabbi Abraham ben Eliezer

The Sanctification of God in Love

Halevi to his spiritual forebears, and his own capacity
to reveal the utter depths of faith, where love and death
embrace in passion.

The use of textual models and exegetical citations has
an ancient role in the representation of suffering
in Jewish sources – and in particular in our theme of
suffering for love of God unto death. Rabbi Abraham's
dependence on ibn Sahula's interpretation of the Song
of Songs points to the powerful influence of that scroll
on the martyrological mentality and imagination of the
Jews. This cannot be overstressed. In a textual culture
like Judaism, the ongoing pedagogy of great texts on
the spiritual physiognomy of the people, and the living
examples of saints who dramatized their contents in full
view, are its life force. It will therefore be instructive to
go back to several ancient sources where verses from the
Song of Songs serve to cultivate the ideal of divine love we
are concerned with. As one literary model interlocks with
another, there gradually emerge martyrological legends
of incalculable influence.

We begin with a tradition reported in the *Mekhilta de-
Rabbi Ishmael* in the name of Rabbi Akiba. By Rabbi
Akiba's time, the notion of sanctification of the divine
Name was undergoing a decisive shift – away from the
more general ideal of giving public honor to God and
Judaism (its norms and *mitzvot*) and toward the exclusive
commitment of martyrdom.[13] In the process, the ideal
of love assumes a privileged position, and again notably
around the figure of Akiba.[14] Only a portion of this
important religious development can be reviewed here;
and within that, we shall focus predominantly on the use
of scriptural citations that establish and generate a spiritual
tradition in its own right.

The Sanctification of God in Love

An instructive beginning is the aforenoted tradition in the *Mekhilta*.[15] Its point of departure is the verse "This is my God and I will glorify Him," from the Song of the Sea (Exodus 15:2). Focusing on the demonstrative pronoun "this," an earlier comment by Rabbi Abraham reports a tradition that the people – all of them – had a vision of their saving Lord at the Sea and, without hesitation, recognized His divinity, saying, "*This* (one) is my God!" Such a motif of recognition, along with praise, is well known in contemporary Roman sources describing the popular *acclamatio* with which the populace greeted the touring emperor. And it is just this feature which Rabbi Akiba utilizes in his scriptural interpretation.

I shall speak of the glory and praises of Him, Who spoke and the world came into being, before all the nations of the world. For the nations of the world ask Israel: "'How is your Beloved greater than any other, that you have thus forsworn [against] us?' [Songs 5:9], since you are ready to die for Him [*metim 'alav*] and be killed for His sake [*neheragin 'alav*]? For it is said: 'Therefore do the maidens [*'alamot*] love You' [Songs 1:3], [meaning] love you unto death [*'ad mavet*];[16] and it is written: 'For your sake [*'alekha*] we are killed [*horagnu*] all day long' [Psalm 44:23]. Truly you are handsome and mighty; come and intermingle with us." But Israel says to the nations of the world: "Do you know Him? Let us tell you some of His praise: 'My Beloved is clear-skinned and ruddy, preeminent over ten thousand' [Songs 5:10], etc." As soon as the nations of the world hear some of His praise, they say to Israel: "We shall join you; as is said: 'Where has your Beloved gone, O fairest of women, and shall we seek Him with you?'" [Songs 6:1]. But Israel responds to the nations of the world: "You can have no share in Him, for 'My Beloved is mine and I am His' [Songs 2:16], 'I am my Beloved's and my Beloved is mine'" [Songs 6:3].

The Sanctification of God in Love

At the outset, Akiba does not so much concentrate on the pronoun "this" as on the rest of the proclamation, "and I shall glorify Him" (*ve-'anvehu*), which he takes to be an assertion of allegiance and loyalty. For Jews in his day, it represents a steadfast commitment to Judaism before the nations of the world. He then proceeds to dramatize the point through a dialogue between Jews and gentiles constructed from verses in the Song of Songs. This is surely an artifice, but a most instructive one. The dialogue begins with the nations – presumably the Romans, who were offended at the exclusivist tendencies of the Jews in their territories, whose religious loyalties were deemed disloyal to Roman civility. These nations ask Israel just who their God is that they remain apart, swearing exclusive fealty. The question has all the puzzlement of the polytheist before a monotheist. Indeed, the puzzlement extends to wondering about a commitment that leads to death in love. Here the query of the nations is cleverly formulated to set up biblical proofs, which are cited in accord with their reinterpreted sense.[17] The verse from Songs 1:3 ("therefore do the maidens love You") is central here, for it first invokes the rabbinic understanding of Israel as the female lover (*'alamot*) of God and then transfigures that image in terms of transcendent death (*'ad mavet*). Going further, the nations glorify the masculinity and bravery of the people and ask them to mingle with them as good Roman citizens. But here the dialogue undergoes a decisive shift. Picking up the query from Songs 5:9, Akiba has Israel now tell the nations a bit of the divine glory (*ne'otav*) through a citation of the physical description of the lover in Songs 5:10–16. The choice is clever, for (the mystic) Akiba does not use these verses in order to show how the parts of the body were reinterpreted in the Midrash to refer to the

The Sanctification of God in Love

Torah or even to hint that just these verses were also the subject of profound mystical speculations about the Divine Anthropos.[18] As distinct from the nomism of the first and the metanomism of the second interpretation, Akiba merely stresses the aesthetic perfection of this God to whom Israel swears loyalty. "This" is only "some" of the divine glory, to be sure; but to Romans enamored with the perfections of physical form the beautiful male described in Songs 5:10–16 puts them in thrall. Such a god is worth adoring, they acclaim, and invoke Songs 6:1 in their bid to join the community of Israel. The tables are now turned, and the dialogue ends with Israel's insistence (via Songs 6:3) on her separateness and special relation to her Beloved God. The final joust alludes to the possessive pronoun in the proclamation "This is *my* God!" and completes Akiba's revision of each element of Exodus 15:2a ("this is"; "my God"; and "I shall glorify Him").

One can only imagine the intense conditions during the time of Hadrian's edicts and persecutions (132–35 C.E.) that could have evoked such a midrashic construction and the monotheistic (and perhaps mystical) fervor that could have inspired the death-defying loyalty of the Jews. The transformation of Songs 6:3 from a proclamation of covenantal love into a climax of devotion is remarkable – the result of a developing sensibility which scorned the sensations of the body for the spirituality of the heart. No wonder the Romans were perplexed; and no wonder, too, that Rabbi Akiba had to invoke an account of a consummate divine beauty to justify such commitment. But for other Jews – equally committed to monotheistic loyalty – the flagrant contempt for physical life flew in the face of other rabbinic values. Thus in a crucial talmudic formulation we learn: "If a gentile demanded of a Jew that he transgress any one of all the commandments stated

The Sanctification of God in Love

in the Torah, with the exception of idolatry, incest, and bloodshed, he should transgress and not [allow himself to] be killed" (*b. Sanhedrin* 74*b*). This statement was intended to restrict uncompromising resistance to a minimum, given the biblical principle that the commandments were given for "life" (Leviticus 18:5) and the rabbinic principle that one cannot deal wantonly with one's body (*M. Baba Qama* VIII.6). Accordingly, the sages discussed whether it made any difference if such acts were performed in private or in public; and in fact, basing himself on the phrase "You shall live by them" (Leviticus 18:5), Rabbi Ishmael even suggested that private acts of idolatry (to save one's life) were allowed but that public displays were not, since Scripture says: "You shall not desecrate My Holy Name, and I shall be sanctified *among* the people of Israel" (Leviticus 22:32).[19] The ancient sages and their medieval heirs went on to make further distinctions concerning conditions of coercion, times of persecution, and the fear of pain. But these merely highlight the basic tension at stake – life against death – and define which acts truly sanctify God.

The development of cultural models of spiritual resistance tempered and transformed old ideals. We have just examined some reworkings of the Song of Songs which served to project the pathos of uncompromising love across the generations. Other verses were reworked as well, such as Songs 2:7, in which the lover adjures her maiden friends "by the gazelles and hinds of the field" because she (Israel) "pours forth her blood for the sanctification of the Name like the blood of gazelles and hinds";[20] Songs 5:2, in which the lover is called "my dove, my pure one" (*tammati*) because she (Israel) is utterly identified (*mut'amim*) with the Holy One and dies for the sanctification of His Name;[21] Songs 5:8, in which the lover says she is "love sick" for her Beloved because she pines for God's love "unto death," as confirmed by Songs 1:3 ("therefore do the maidens love You") and 8:6 ("for love is as strong as death");[22] and Songs 7:8–9, in which those resisting idolatry are praised for standing "erect [*domim*] as palms" for God says that He will be "glorified [*mit'alleh*] by the palm [Israel]" on the basis of the praise of the lover by the Beloved ("your stature is like [*dameta*] a palm") and his own assertion that he will "climb [*'e'eleh*] the palm" in love.[23] All these comments combined to specify the ideal of sanctified love through death from late Tannaitic times (the period of Hadrian) on. Indeed, through both the rabbinic curriculum and the agency of key commentators (like Rashi's elaboration of the foregoing interpretation of Songs 7:7–8), these "textual events" became models for imitation – conditioning historical events on the basis of their exegetical representation of reality.

Two lines of evidence support this point. The first concerns the persecution of the Jews in 167–166 B.C.E., during the reign of Antiochus Epiphanes IV. According to 2 Maccabees 7:1–42 and 4 Maccabees 6–18, two exemplary acts of spiritual resistance occurred at that time: the heroic death of the elder Eleazar and the deaths of a mother and her seven sons (at Antioch).[24] All were ordered to worship idols or die, and all died "nobly for piety's sake"; for "only those who with all their heart make piety their first concern are able to conquer the passions of the flesh, believing that to God they do not die (as our patriarchs Abraham, Isaac, and Jacob died not) but live to God" (4 Maccabees 6:22, 7:18–19). Indeed, at death each one of the martyrs delivered a speech replete with Greek ideals of piety (culled in part from Plato's *Gorgias*).[25] Each exhorted the other to "fight for the sacred," maintain "constancy," and leave behind a

The Sanctification of God in Love

"heroic example and a glorious memory." Nothing is mentioned here of the martyrs' contempt for idolatry or paganism, nor is there use of scriptural citations – in contrast to the way the "event" entered the Jewish historical imagination via the midrashic literature. [26] Indeed, the screen of Greek rhetoric is now torn aside and the passion of the mother (called Miriam bat Tanḥum) and her sons draws from accounts of Jewish suffering in the days of Hadrian. The claim that this revision is due to an ideological change in the notion of martyrdom must be revised in light of the stronger evidence in favor of the influence of another literary genre: pagan and Christian martyrological literature of the third to fourth centuries (C.E.). [27] Since there were no Jewish persecutions at that time, [28] we are left with the paradoxical but inescapable conclusion that this influential tableau of martyrdom entered the Jewish spiritual imagination through an alien filter. The rabbis drew on the acts of martyrs known to them (in real life or literature) in order to give a historical character to their reports. But what they have done is trade one rhetorical representation of reality (the Hellenic) for another (pagan and Christian). The end result is the creation of a martyrological myth whose origins were long forgotten.

The same holds true for the death of Rabbi Akiba, and the result is more compelling, given the typological role his martyrdom has played in the religious memory and practice of Jews. This centrality justifies a somewhat extended evaluation of the evidence. Most famous is the scene reported in the Babylonian Talmud (*b. Berakhot* 61*b*):

When Rabbi Akiba was taken out for execution, it was the hour for recital of the Shema [the credo of divine unity;

The Sanctification of God in Love

Deuteronomy 6:4]; and while they [the Romans] raked his flesh with iron combs, he was accepting upon himself the Kingship of Heaven. His disciples said to him: "Our master, even to this point [will you accept suffering]?" He answered them: "My whole life I have been troubled by this verse 'with all your soul' [from Deuteronomy 6:5], [which means:] even if He takes your soul. I wondered if I should have the opportunity to fulfill it; and now that I do, shall I not fulfill it?" [And so] he prolonged reciting the [final] word "One" [of the credo: "Hear, O Israel! The Lord is our God, the Lord is One"], until his soul departed with [the word] "One."

In this tableau of torture and transcendence, Akiba dies in "exegetical ecstasy," so to speak, fulfilling a verse of Scripture according to a martyrological interpretation of it. To love God with all one's soul is to love Him unto death, even if He takes one's soul. This interpretation is also found in the earlier *Testament of Dan* (5:3), where one is enjoined to "love" God "with all your life"; as well as in a teaching of Akiba's master, Rabbi Meir, who earlier explained the phrase to mean "even if He takes your soul" (*Sifrei Deuteronomy* 32). The Mishnah (*M. Berakhot* IX.5) provides the same explanation in connection with the exhortation to bless evil happenings along with the good ones. And so, Rabbi Akiba not only recites the prayer of divine unity at his death but does so to fulfill a rabbinic teaching that he wholeheartedly accepted. Word and deed are thus consummated together: the sage expires in perfection.

Such is the great scene as it inspired millennia. But it leaves a lot to wonder about.[29] Although the immediate setting indicates punishment for teaching the Torah in groups, against government decree, the overall context is a series of exegetical comments on Deuteronomy 6:5.

The Sanctification of God in Love

Akiba's martyrology thus appears to be, in part, a living exemplification of exegesis. Indeed, the sage even teaches his interpretation of the verse during his torture. Not only that, it would even appear that he interrupts his recitation of the Shema (quite against halakhic regulations) in order to answer the students' query – for after explaining his motivation for such constancy in suffering (based on v. 6), the saint returned to the liturgy and prolonged his enunciation of the final word until his life-breath gave out. In this regard, one must note that *only* Akiba's recitation is time determined (as liturgically required). There is no suggestion that his persecution was caused by that proclamation of faith.

The version in the Jerusalem Talmud makes more sense. Here is the account in *j. Soṭa* 5.20c:

Rabbi Akiba was prosecuted by the evil Tinneius Rufus when the time for reciting the Shema approached. He [thus] began the recitation and laughed. Rufus queried: "Old man! Are you a wizard or scoffer at sufferings?" Akiba answered: "Blast you! I'm neither a wizard nor scoffer at sufferings. But my whole life I have read this verse . . . 'You shall love the Lord your God with all your heart and with all your soul and with all your might.' [Now] I have loved him with all my heart and all my wealth, but I never had the occasion to [fulfill the phrase] 'and with all your soul.' And now that this opportunity has arisen at the time for reciting the Shema, I shall not miss it. Therefore I recited [it] and laughed." Akiba didn't get to finish when his soul departed.

The difference between this report and the one in the Babylonian tradition lies in the more plausible sequence of events and motivations. It now appears that Akiba disrupted the legal proceeding with a flagrant act of resistance to the pagan authorities.[30] Turning from his prosecutor, he proclaimed God's unity and kingdom with joy, thus implicitly denying the divinity of the emperor and the authority of his realm.[31] Torture must then have followed this protest, during which Akiba seemed inured to pain. Astounded, Tinneius Rufus thought him a wizard; but the saint dismissed this nonsense and answered in terms of his ideal of perfected love. It is an honest answer conveying his personal exegesis of the verse. He meant no disrespect; and surely, he suggests, his laugh is neither an incantation nor an expression of contempt. Much more is it the joy of obedience, a transfigured joy that allows Akiba to transcend physical pain. But tortured he was, and sorely so; for he died before completing the recitation. Since there is no suggestion that he interrupted the opening line (the dialogue seems to follow the proclamation), we may conclude that Akiba did say "the Lord is One" – the offending declaration – and died before completing the subsequent paragraphs of the Shema. Alternatively, Akiba was not able to complete his answer to the authority before expiring. Either way, he died of his wounds after a consummate expression of defiance and devotion.

What then produced the martyrology of *b. Berakhot* 61*b*, in which the saint is queried by his disciples (not Tinneius Rufus) and his soul departs while enunciating God's unity? The answer may lie in a series of exegetical-homiletical considerations. Note first that Akiba's exegesis of the phrase "with all your soul" is given to his disciples, in what constitutes an impromptu study session. Given that Akiba was arrested for teaching in public assemblies, the event bristles with irony. With utter contempt for the authorities, the Babylonian version has him instruct his students at the very hour of his death! What is more, this account totally ignores the kingdom of evil and its representatives and focuses entirely on Akiba's acceptance of the Kingdom of Heaven. The narrative is thus designed for instruction – a stylized martyrology to inspire imitation. The concluding coda (not quoted above) reinforces this point. After the saint's death a heavenly voice asserts that Akiba has earned life in the World to Come. The message to the faithful is clear.

There is another stylized feature of this martyrology, which transforms Akiba's declaration of divine unity into a "last word and testament." Circumstances aside, our ancient sources show several literary patterns for the death of a sage. In one of them, the master dies with a characteristic or emblematic word on his lips. Thus in one instance, Ben Dama (the son of Rabbi Ishmael's sister) was bitten by a serpent and wished to be healed by Jacob of Kefar Sekania. He was forbidden to do so by Rabbi Ishmael, in accord with the ruling (of which this episode provides a case in point) that "no man should have any dealings with *minim* [heretics], nor is it allowed to be healed by them even [to prolong] life for an hour." Ben Dama protested and even claimed that he could prove from Scripture that this was permitted. "But he was not able to finish the matter when his soul departed and he died." In response, Rabbi Ishmael said: "How fortunate are you, Ben Dama," for he died "in purity" without transgressing his colleagues' ruling.[32] In a second case, several students came before Rabbi Eliezer on his deathbed for instruction on a series of halakhic difficulties dealing with matters of purity. Being an expert, the sage answered each one in turn. At the query of Rabbi Eleazar ben Azariah, concerning a shoe on a last, the sage answered, "'pure,' and his soul departed in purity."[33]

Taken together, these two cases illustrate the literary pattern that conditions the representation of Akiba's death in *b. Berakhot 61b*. Like the first case, Akiba was in the midst of a declaration when he died and inspired the comment "How fortunate"; and like the second one, the sage died enunciating a phrase which characterized his rabbinical life. Clearly we have to do with an exemplary death scene of sorts and should not infer historical specifics without due caution. Indeed, by means of the several stylistic elements discussed so far, the realistic events of Akiba's prosecution and torture have become legendary. Their mythic proportions took effect as the scene was studied for the sake of spiritual merit or imitation. For example, the talmudic hagiography burgeons into the larger-than-life legend of the "Ten Martyrs," known colloquially as the *Eleh Ezkerah*, a late Byzantine martyrology in which a variety of sages die for the sanctification of the divine Name and atone for an ancient delict. [34] Although Akiba is but one saint among many, his heroic death decisively influenced the portrayal of others. This is notably evident in the recension (Vatican MS. Ebr. 285) of *Eleh Ezkerah* in which the soul of Rabbi Eleazar ben Shamua departs at the word "God" while sanctifying the Sabbath (Genesis 2:3) and in which Rabbi Yeshebab the Scribe expires at the word "and [God] said" in the final paragraph of the Shema (Numbers 15:37), and also in the many instances where the deaths of the martyrs evoke the refrain "How fortunate are you" and the promise of an eternal reward in heaven. [35] The events of history thus pass into the realm of mimesis – a realm of imitation and representation in which myth is born.

The literary shaping of martyrological events serves a double purpose: it instructs the culture in models of spiritual resistance and provides dramatic examples of sanctification whereby these acts could be inscribed in cultural memory. Indeed, the historicity of these examples

The Sanctification of God in Love

(in the strict sense) is less important than the tradition of pious behavior transmitted. The rhetoric of literary models thus invokes a mythic moment, foundational for religious memory; just as the recitation of this content (in study or prayer) has a liturgical dimension that exalts the martyrs (*qedoshim ve-niśrafim*) and idealizes the merit of their deeds. Such inspirational hagiography invigorates history with the truth of faith, projecting patterns of piety that reveal the nerve of monotheistic fidelity. The following is a case in point. It derives from the so-called *Chronicle of Solomon bar Simson* (a twelfth-century account of the First Crusade) and presents an event in Mainz in 1096.[36]

When the people of the Holy Covenant saw that the [divine] decree was sealed, and that the enemy had vanquished them and entered the courtyard, they cried altogether – elders and youths, virgins and babes, and male and female servants – to their heavenly Father and bewailed themselves and their lives. And they accepted the judgment of Heaven, and said to each other: "Let us be strong and suffer the yoke of holy reverence. For [though] our enemies will kill us for the span of an hour, and by the easiest form [death by sword], our souls will live forever in the Garden of Eden. . . ." And they said with whole hearts and willing souls: "The ultimate point is not to ponder the ways of the Holy One, blessed be He, and blessed be His Name, who has given us His Torah and commanded us to allow ourselves to be killed and slain for the unity of His holy Name. Fortunate are we, if we do His will; and fortunate is he who is slain or slaughtered or dies for the unity of His Name – for he is destined for the world to come and will dwell among the righteous, *with Rabbi Akiba and his colleagues, the pillars of the world, who were slain for His Name*."

As the italicized portion indicates, Rabbi Akiba and his fellow martyrs – as reported in the Talmud and the

The Sanctification of God in Love

Midrash *Eleh Ezkerah* – were the model held before the masses in this exhortation to die for the sanctification of God. But the nuanced allusions of the rhetoric deserve closer attention, since they clearly reveal what I have called the exegetical construction of reality. This is not to say that the *Chronicle* is without historical "fact" and "information" but to concur with those who argue that the "local Jewish chronicles and hagiographies . . . are not documentary records to which theological comments and poems have been added [but rather] highly edited, rhetorically colored, and liturgically motivated literary reworkings of circular letters and oral reports, written for definite purposes."37 Thus, not only does the phrase "the [divine] decree was sealed" (*nigzerah ha-gezerah*) recall a key phrase in *Eleh Ezkerah* (Rabbi Ishmael ascends to heaven to learn if the martyrology is *divinely* determined),38 but other phrases allude to *b. Berakhot* 61*b* (and thence *Eleh Ezkerah*) along with other Akiba traditions. Thus, the words "fortunate are we" and "destined [*mezumman*] for the world to come" evoke the angelic coda at the end of the talmudic account, even as the people's commitment of their "whole hearts and willing souls" recalls Akiba's reading of Deuteronomy 6:5. The people also determine not to ponder the "ways" (*middah*) of God. This was Rabbi Akiba's interpretation of the phrase "with all your might," as preserved in *Sifrei Deuteronomy* 32.39 Playing on the word *me'od* (might), he said that one should accept with faithful equanimity "every occurrence [lit., "measure"; *middah*] which God metes out [*moddedin*]." Not citing Akiba, the Mishnah (*Berakhot* IX.5) concurs: "with all your might – for every measure [*middah u-middah*] which [God] metes out [*moded*] to you, praise [*modeh*] Him greatly [*be-me'od me'od*]."

73

The Sanctification of God in Love

There can be little doubt, therefore, that Solomon bar Simson's chronicle employs exegetical constructions that give mythic dimensions to the martyrs of Mainz. Its purpose (in part) was to assimilate their deeds to those of the ancient saints and thus add a new chapter to Israel's genealogy of suffering. But what would be the case when such acts of religious constancy and conviction were not performed in the flesh? How was the memory of the martyrs maintained and ritualized as an enduring model of love of God? One means was study; another was daily ritual. Both options are mentioned in the *Yosef 'Ometz,* a collection of liturgical and other practices written by Rabbi Yosef Yuzpe Hahn (Nordlingen), who lived in the sixteenth and seventeenth centuries (1570–1635) and witnessed the Fettmilch massacres. Citing a passage from Rabbi Yosselman Rosheim, the great Court Jew (d. 1554), in which the rules of martyrology are mentioned along with a stirring exhortation to fulfill the commandment,[40] Hahn urges his readers to learn the rules well so that there would be no danger of dying unnecessarily, for then one would be guilty of suicide and not praiseworthy for sanctifying God's Name in love.[41] It has been argued that this emphasis on study is one facet of a seventeenth-century transformation in the meaning of Jewish martyrdom, the others being an absence of contemptuous resistance to Christianity (common in the twelfth-century martyrologies) and a new emphasis on ritual spiritualization of the sanctification.[42]

The argument is not without difficulty since, in the first case, considerations of the proper conditions for "putting one's life at risk" were long a part of the talmudic curriculum and of the posttalmudic annotators and decisors.[43] Study of these "rules of sanctification" constituted an authentic part of rabbinic piety, vitally concerned with

knowing the commandments and their proper performance. The very fact that such behavior (not to mention
a précis of related rules[44]) is prescribed in a book whose
genre conforms with others dealing with customs and
ritual should give double pause. And if the matter of
genre is significant here, it must also temper any inference
about active resistance to be drawn from *Yosef 'Ometz*,
for it hardly helps to compare twelfth-century chronicles
with a seventeenth-century book of ritual instructions.
Indeed, if one were to turn to the chronicles of Hahn's
day, such as the *Yevein Metzula* of Rabbi Nathan Neta
Hanover, one can find many exhortations of religious
constancy and defiance. The case in Tulczyn may stand
for many. According to the chronicler, the great scholars
of that city "urged the holy people to sanctify the Name
and not to change their faith. [And] all of them replied:
'Hear O Israel, the Lord is our God, the Lord is One! As
there is but One in your hearts, so is there but One in
our hearts.'" And when the enemy came and proclaimed,
"Whoever wishes to change his faith and remain alive,
let him sit under this banner," none answered and many
were killed mercilessly.[45]

The third contention bears directly on our subject.
It claims that the focus on ritual performance reflects a
decisive spiritualization of martyrology – a shift from
concrete action (real death) to mental substitution, at a
time when Christianity was no longer the same aggressive
threat to the Jew that it had been in medieval Europe.
But we must be careful not to misjudge this interior
ritualization of self-sacrifice during normal circumstances.
Hahn's discussion is instructive.

In addition to this [foregoing] reason [for learning the rules
of martyrdom], there is, in my opinion, a greater one: that a

person should learn those laws upon which the foundation of our faith depends; for [their very name proves this, since] they are called [the laws for the] sanctification of the Name. Accordingly, whoever studies them in all their details and devotes himself in love for the sanctification of His great Name, then this theoretical recollection and acceptance will be considered as a deed in fact – in accordance with what the sages have said concerning whoever studies the [biblical] portion of sacrifices . . . and the wise among the Kabbalists assert likewise. . . . Because there are indeed a number of commandments that certain persons will never be obligated to perform, these will be accounted in his favor if he [but] studies their laws and affirms to fulfill them if necessary. . . . This acceptance will be deemed a deed in fact. In just this way did the sages expound the [biblical] verse "For Your sake are we killed all day long" in the [Midrash] *Sifrei,* [saying,] "And is it conceivable that one be killed every day? Rather, [the sense is] that should one accept upon himself daily to sanctify His great Name, it will be accounted as [if he were] a sheep [led] to the slaughter"; see *Sefer Ḥaredim* 17, which cites the *Zohar* that everyone should accept upon himself self-sacrifice [*mesirut nafsho*] for the sanctification of the Name through elongating the word "One" [in the Shema], and also when he recites "with all your heart and all your soul."[46]

In a document of such import, it would be unduly captious to conclude that the substitutions for martyrdom indicated here are merely historical displacements, without concrete religious value. Granted, Rabbi Yosef Hahn cites an old rabbinic dictum (from *b. Menaḥot* 110*a*) that vaunts the merit of studying the laws of sacrifice after the destruction of the Temple; but it is hard to say if this is merely a homiletical hyperbole or a real shift in the meaning of vicarious substitution for the rabbis. Whatever the case, the medieval Kabbalists took this dictum

The Sanctification of God in Love

seriously, as Hahn himself notes, and the reason he gives is significant: substitution is necessary to enable one to fulfill those commandments – like sacrifice – which would otherwise be impossible to fulfill owing to historical circumstances. That is to say, though the commandment to sanctify God's Name is one of the positive duties of the Halakhah, there are various conditions attached to its physical performance (even in times of persecution) such that one may never have the opportunity to show selfless devotion to God or observe *all* the *mitzvot*. For the traditional Jew this was no light matter. And so we find Rabbi Yosef Hahn drawing on ancient midrashic sources, the thirteenth-century *Zohar* and the sixteenth-century *Sefer Ḥaredim* – all for the purpose of teaching that one may also fulfill the *mitzvah* of sanctifying God's Name through the proper recitation of the Shema; that is, one must recite the opening proclamation of unity and the succeeding determination to love God with "all your soul" with absolute sincerity. Since the last clause was undoubtedly understood in the Akiban sense, "even if He takes your soul," the requirement is that one should recite the prayer *as if (ke'ilu)* one were giving up one's soul at that very moment (and also intending to do so in fact, circumstances permitting). Performed this way, the verbal utterance would fulfill the physical *mitzvah*.

I shall return at greater length to the issue of ritual substitutions and performance in the final chapter. For now it will suffice to consider just what lies behind the emphasis on fulfilling this commandment, even in vicarious form. The desire to fulfill all of the commandments was already mentioned. But what theological reasons are involved? Two significant answers may be adduced. The first of these occurs in another portion of the *Yosef 'Ometz* passage. After Hahn's comment that one who studies the laws of sanctification of the Name has the merit of one who has actually performed the commandment, he adds: "And the wise among the Kabbalists assert likewise." The rest of the remark continues as follows:

And the wise among the Kabbalists assert likewise in response to a problem raised in connection with the transmigration of souls. They [the Kabbalists] said that a person could not acquire perfection without fulfilling [all of] the 613 commandments; and were he to omit even one of the commandments of God his supernal garment would be wanting, and he would have to return to the round of rebirth until he had performed all 613 commandments. Against this, it was objected: "Now surely there are a number of commandments that a person might never have the opportunity to perform." And they [the Kabbalists] answered: "If one were to study such laws, and determine to fulfill them if the occasion should arise . . . this [theoretical] acceptance would be accounted a deed in fact."

This text transports us into the world of mystical metempsychosis – of the transmigration of souls – in which the perfect performance of all the commandments is required for release from the cycle of rebirth. According to this Kabbalistic notion, found variously in the *Zohar* (but of great antiquity; cf. *Ascension of Isaiah* 8:14–15; 9:1–5, 36–40), each completed commandment adds a piece to the supernal garment that a person weaves upon his astral body.[47] Failure to fully clothe one's heavenly alter ego results in a deficit that returns the earth-bound soul to the travails of rebirth. It was therefore necessary for those who accepted this Kabbalistic tradition to find a means for performing *all* the commandments.[48] For the *mitzvah* of sanctification of God's Name, the solution provided was ritual study of the rules of martyrdom and proper martyrological meditations – the readiness to die for love of God – during prayer.

Another good reason may be offered for the importance of actualizing martyrdom during worship. For this we must return to the *Megillat Amraphel* of Rabbi Abraham ben Eliezer Halevi. That discourse began with a recitation of the dictum that a person should wholeheartedly determine to take on the rite of sanctification, and it invokes the technique of envisioning the holy Name of God during torture. At the conclusion of the text comes the martyrological commentary on the Song of Songs. Between these two paragraphs there is a section dealing with a different aspect of our theme. It makes use of several phrases and texts considered so far – with one arresting addition. Rabbi Abraham says:

It is also of value to know, to make known, and to be aware [of the fact] that if a person recites the Shema both morning and eve and sets his mind with a correct and focused intention when he recites the love of God's Name and its unity, and determines in his heart [*gomer be-libbo*] to devote to Him his body and soul and wife and children and to love Him with all his heart and all his soul and all his might, even when he prostrates himself in prayer, after he has stood alive during the Amidah prayer, and to confess his sins and say, "I commit my soul to You, O Lord" [Psalm 25:1], and he deposits his soul with his God, and his God bears his soul and spirit and gathers his breath to Himself, as if he were going to his eternal home – truly that person has a share in Life and will go to the Light by the Light of Life, together with the righteous and the pious and the saints who sanctify the Holiness of Jacob and praise the God of Israel. [For such a person] even those sins which would go unatoned until the day of his death are atoned for at that time; for he has truly determined in his heart [*gamar be-libbo*] and devoted

The Sanctification of God in Love

himself to his God as if he were dead [ke'ilu meit], gone and
annihilated from this world. And this is a great thing; for so
the King established, and concerning these things the poet
cried out by the spirit of God, saying, "For Your sake we
are killed all the day, [and] are accounted as sheep brought
for slaughter" [Psalm 44:23].

Here we have, once again, a ritualization of death: a performance of the Shema in wholehearted devotion and the
intent to offer one's soul to God if required. Such a person
practices the ultimate passion daily – during recitation of
the credo and prostration during the penitentials – and
thereby "at that time" is forgiven all his sins, even the
most severe. By such acts a person is "as if" dead, so
wholly has he devoted his soul to God's keeping; and he
can therefore be shriven of sins requiring death itself for
atonement. Ritual dying is thus a mode of purification and
self-transformation. Through the model of the martyrs,
liturgy imitates life – exegesis and all. I shall return to
this subject in the final chapter.

Two further texts bring our theme to new spiritual
heights. The first comes from the 'Avodat ha-Qodesh,
a sixteenth-century Kabbalistic compendium by Rabbi
Meir ibn Gabbai. Speaking of the spiritual end of a "lover"
of the divine "Companion" (re'a), ibn Gabbai teaches
that one must keep far from any evil (ra') that would
separate one from God (re'a), and maintain one's heart
in a state of perfect unity (yihud). This devoted service,
which results in mystical union with God, is "the great
principle of the Torah" as taught by Rabbi Akiba in his
maxim "You shall love your neighbor [re'a] as yourself:
this is a great principle of the Torah." For that sage, the
true re'a is God; and the most perfect expression of human

The Sanctification of God in Love

love for God, until He is "as yourself" in transcendental union, is the act of sanctifying His Name in martyrdom. In fulfillment of his own exegesis,

Rabbi Akiba . . . devoted himself to the sanctification of the Name out of love, this being the most complete unity, for his soul departed at "One." And this [was done] for the sake of perfection, since by his spirit and soul he came to perfect the end of the [gradation of] supernal thought – and this is the mystery of sanctity and unity; and by his body he "sweetened" the enclosure of Thought . . . – and this is like the mystery of the sacrifices known to the wise of heart [Kabbalists]. And his heart was not divided within him, but unified in all its parts. And he thereby sanctified the Name, as is said, "And I shall be sanctified among the people of Israel" [Leviticus 22:32]. And this is the [true] "beloved companion [re'a]"; for [out of love for God he] is [religiously] scrupulous and hates what his Companion [re'ehu] hates and does not desecrate His Name, as in the matter "And you shall not desecrate My holy Name" [Leviticus 22:32]. And thus the love of the companion [re'a] for his Companion [re'ehu] should go so far as to remove the division which separates them, [so as] to be present with Him "face to face" and to cleave to Him steadfastly. And for this reason he should devote his body, which impedes this conjunction, to be sacrificed before Him; and then his spirit shall cleave to the spirit of his Companion [re'ehu], "the one touching [mashiqot] the Other" [Ezekiel 3:13]. And the two [of them] will then be one entity (kelal); and this is [the true meaning of the phrase] "a great principle [kelal] in the Torah."[49]

This powerful text turns on a mystical reading of the biblical exhortation "You shall love your neighbor [re'a] as yourself" (Leviticus 19:18), in light of Rabbi Akiba's rabbinic maxim about this being "a great principle in the

The Sanctification of God in Love

Torah." The neighbor is the divine Companion who is loved until He become "as yourself" in the rapture of unity (*kelal*). For ibn Gabbai, Akiba himself achieved this great goal through martyrdom, when his spirit joined the divine and all bodily impediments were removed. Indeed, this act of devotion and cleaving is not just a perfection of the human being but a (theurgical) perfection of the supernal Being itself. Absolute annihilation of the self is thus a return to the divine Whole (*kelal*) and a reparation of it through the ultimate human sacrifice. Drawing on the *Zohar*'s reuse of Songs 1:2, in which the kisses (*neshiqot*) of the mouth are the sharing of spirit (*ruaḥ*) or breath,[50] and on the old midrashic interpretation of *neshiqot* as spiritual cleaving (*mashiqot*),[51] ibn Gabbai has transfigured the climax of religious devotion (martyrdom) in terms of an ultimate kiss.

The second spiritualization of our subject comes from the Hasidic work *'Arvei Naḥal*, a Torah commentary by Rabbi David Shelomo Eybeschuetz of Soroki (1755–1813).[52] In it a number of themes dealt with in this chapter come to reexpression around the figure of Rabbi Akiba and his martyrdom. Indeed, the text takes its point of departure from a problem arising in the account of the saint's torture found in *b. Menaḥot 29b*. In the classic version (*b. Berakhot 61b*), the angels see Akiba's flesh raked with combs and shout, "Is this the reward for [a life devoted to] Torah?" God tells them that Akiba is destined for an eternal reward. In *b. Menaḥot* it is Moses (during a heavenly ascent) who is given a preview of Akiba's suffering and complains, "Is this the reward for [a life devoted to] Torah?" He is answered by God, "Silence, [for] so has it arisen in [My] thought!"[53] Rabbi Eybeschuetz goes on to say that this divine response is quite astonishing and needs to be explained.

The Sanctification of God in Love

He begins his explanation by saying that a person who daily takes upon himself the Kingdom of Heaven in the Shema prayer "and devotes himself enthusiastically *in his thought* to be slain for the sanctification of the Name has much bliss at such moments," because he is only imagining this death in his thought and is not undergoing the torture in actuality. The reason for this is that "the world of Thought is utterly cut off from [the world of] physical sensations." Nevertheless,

[i]t is written in a responsum of Rabbi Meir of Rothenberg that there is an oral tradition that one who is slain for the honor of the blessed Name feels no pain at all. And the reason is that when such a one goes forth to be slain, enflamed by a powerful desire to die for the sake of His blessed Name, he raises up all his feelings and sensations through that fervor to the world of Thought, until he is entirely absorbed in Thought, such that his feelings are nullified and his bodily sensations are stripped away. Thus he only feels joy, like the one who is burnt [only] in [his] thought.

Thus it also was with Rabbi Akiba, says Rabbi Eybeschuetz, whose bliss increased in proportion to the tortures perpetrated upon him. His companions then realized that he was beyond suffering and that God was not bringing torment upon him but only pleasure; and for this they (positively) exclaimed: "This [surely] is the true reward for [a life devoted to] Torah!"54 God then answered and confirmed the marvel, saying: "'Thus [he] went up [into] Thought!' That is to say, so much did Rabbi Akiba raise his feelings and sensations and corporeality into the [supernatural] world of Thought" that he completely transcended earthly pain and experienced only the highest bliss.

The Sanctification of God in Love

This is a remarkable theodicy, transforming rebuke for apparent divine injustice into an exclamation of praise, and the seemingly abrasive divine dismissal of the protest into a teaching of theosophical mysteries. Akiba thus becomes the prototype of the martyrs who transcended torture and an exemplar of the quietistic theology of the school of the Maggid of Mezeritzch.[55] Absorbed in a state of transcendental consciousness amid the sufferings of this world, Rabbi Akiba is also the model for all those who "practice" such absolute devotion in the course of their daily worship. Such practices were mentioned in connection with the teachings of the *Yosef 'Ometz*. They will be the subject of chapter 3.

I would conclude with two transformations of the motif of death by divine kiss as it relates to martyrology. The first is found in an old midrash on the Book of Lamentations (though a variant is found in the Talmud as well) and gives an almost cherubic transfiguration of our theme.[56] The account states that after the destruction of the Temple in 70 c.e., two children of High Priest Zadok were taken captive by two Roman officers. The boy was sold by one of them to a whore for the price of his pleasure; and the girl was sold by his compatriot for wine. Some time later, the whore and the innkeeper struck a deal. They married off the pair in hopes of breeding them for profit. Thereupon, the siblings were placed in a room alone. The girl began to cry and, to the boy's query as to her sorrow, said that she was crying because she, the daughter of the high priest, had been wed to a mere slave. Whereupon the boy asked her where she had lived, and to give specifics, and also whether she had any brothers and sisters. The girl described her house and neighborhood in Jerusalem and added that she had a brother with a mole on his shoulder, which she used to kiss when he came home from school. The boy then asked her if she could still recognize this birthmark, and when she said yes he bared his shoulder so that they recognized each other. The story concludes with the remark: "They embraced each other and kissed each other until their souls departed."

This little recognition scene by two siblings reflects a widespread folk motif. In our case, it has been transformed and influenced by a skillful play upon a vision of doom given by the prophet Joel, who said, "Then they bartered a boy for a whore, and sold a girl for wine" (Joel 4:3). This doomsday prophecy now serves to dramatize and express the sufferings of the Jewish exile and the faithfulness of the deportees. Once again it is the exegetical construction of reality that marks Jewish memory. The reworking of older motifs goes further, however; for one may readily see that the imagery of martyrological sanctification marks the expiration of the siblings' souls. Like saints before them, the pair die in the rapture of a kiss. Moreover, it is also emphasized that the boy and girl remain chaste. In this way, the ancient rabbinic law requiring that one must die a martyr before transgressing the laws of incest (even in private) has been miraculously observed. To heighten the purity and sanctity portrayed, the simple motif of the sister kissing her brother's birthmark has been transformed here into the kisses of the siblings unto death. Indeed, in their final rapture the entwined pair represent nothing so much as the embrace of the holy Cherubim. According to an old talmudic tradition, this winged pair was entwined in loving embrace in the Holy of Holies.[57] The enraptured death of the children is thus a transfiguration of an ancient angelic harmony: a unification of opposites in exile.

The final text is not as blissful and comes from the nightmare of modern Jewish history in Eastern Europe.

The Sanctification of God in Love

Once again the kiss represents a resistance to tyranny, but in the story by Lamed Shapiro we have the consummate ironization of the motif. In "Der Kush," a tale of terror in *Die Yudishe Melukhe,* the kiss of death is a grotesque act that dramatizes in an almost surrealistic way the crass realism of evil in our times.[58] It tells of one Reb Shakhne, who first appears amid the plunder of a pogrom cowering under a bench, unable to act. It is there that the rabble, the *shekotzim,* find him and drag him out to perform to their drunken delight. And then it happens. One of the rioters, who had been well treated by Reb Shakhne, gets it into his head that the Jew should kiss his foot, and so he gets the holy man down on his knees and waits barefooted. Perhaps it was the degraded position itself, or that it evoked in him the ancient law that one should die a martyr before doing idolatrous service. But there it was, an ultimate moment: the holy Jew with his curled beard bent forward, his ancient face before the stinking red toe of his tormentor. Shapiro gives the encounter mythic dimensions – as also the response of Reb Shakhne. When he acts, he bites the putrid object with cannibalistic fury. The thugs pummel him to a bloody pulp, but the Jew holds on, dying in his resistance. No heavenly voice rescues this story from the curse of history; and no Akiba-like rapture restores this ritual from the fetid swamp of hate. The kiss of death here is an insane act: the Jew dies in the stink of Satan. Of him Scripture says, "For Your sake we are killed all day long."

3

"As if he sacrificed a soul"

Forms of Ritual Simulation
and Substitution

The longing for spiritual fulfillment, so characteristic of the quest for God among philosophers, mystics, and martyrs, is, as we have seen, a loving unto death – a commitment of "all" one's soul to God. This was the ideal to be maintained as much as possible and in whatever way possible. For this reason, ritual replacements were formulated whenever the most supreme commitment could not be made or properly performed. Two types have been mentioned. The first brings us back to the interpretation of Deuteronomy 6:5 found in the Midrash *Sifrei Deuteronomy* 32.[1] Responding to the martyrological application of the phrase "with all your soul" and its elaboration through the psalmist's remark "For Your sake are we killed all day long, and regarded as sheep for the slaughter" (Psalm 44:23), Rabbi Simeon ben Menasia rejected this as a concrete daily ideal ("Is it possible to be killed *all day long*?") and offered an alternative. He said that the passage should rather be taken to mean that God credits the righteous "as if" (*ke'ilu*) they are slain daily for His sake – that is, the deeds of the righteous, who "kill" their evil desires out of devotion to God, are deemed a

Ritual Simulation and Substitution

more spiritualized realization of martyrological values. In this way the disciplined devotion to God through the commandments fulfills the obligation to love God "with all your soul," and makes it practicable. The life-enhancing rituals of the Law thus provide a functional substitute for the absolute practice of death.

The second type of ritual substitution was briefly noted in connection with the *Yosef 'Ometz* of Rabbi Yosef Yuzpe Hahn Nordlingen.[2] Because some commandments, like the duty to sanctify the divine Name, are not always feasible in one's lifetime, a functional equivalent was found ("considered" or "accounted," *neheshav*) in the act of studying the relevant laws and determining to fulfill them if the chance to do so arose. A precedent to this effect was adduced from Rabbi Simeon's interpretation of Psalm 44:23 in the *Sifrei*. Directly alluding to that passage (in which the speaker says that he and his people are "considered" or "accounted," *neheshavnu,* as sheep for the slaughter), Rabbi Yosef Hahn remarks that one who "determines daily to sanctify His great Name" by reciting Deuteronomy 6:5 with absolute devotion "is accounted [*neheshav*] as a sheep for the slaughter." Since the context deals with the very practical merit accrued by worshippers for the sake of their perfection and release from rebirth, the actuarial denotation of the verb *neheshav* must be emphasized; that is, it is not merely a matter of God taking note or consideration of these deeds but of actually accruing them to the account of good deeds of the worshipper. Accordingly, it is not only the ascetic discipline of the Jew that is accredited (Rabbi Simeon's view) but the inner determination to sanctify God with all one's soul in prayer and (if necessary) practice. The merit of martyrdom begins in meditation: intention is like the deed, in fact.

Ritual Simulation and Substitution

The issue of ritual substitutions, and in particular the role of study and ascetic self-sacrifice, take us back to the early rabbinic period. A collection of interpretations at the end of the talmudic tractate *b. Menaḥot* (110*a*) is notable in this regard. Each one invokes the expression *ke'ilu* (as if) to note the functional equivalent of Torah study and Temple service. The first two are fairly general: "scholars who devote themselves to the study of Torah wherever they are," or "at night," are accounted "as if" they "burnt and presented offerings" to God or "were occupied with the Temple service." The third more closely specifies that "scholars who are occupied with the laws of the Temple service" are considered "as if the Temple were built in their days." But it is the fourth and fifth interpretations that connect the performative benefits of study with the transformative effects of sacrifices in a detailed way.

Resh Laqish said, "What is the significance of the verse 'This is the law for the burnt-offering, for the meal-offering, for the sin-offering, and for the guilt-offering' [Leviticus 7:37]? It teaches that whoever occupies himself with the study of the Torah is as if [*ke'ilu*] he were offering a burnt-offering, a meal-offering, a sin-offering, and a guilt-offering." Rabba asked, "Why then does the verse say '*for* the burnt-offering, *for* the meal-offering'? It should rather have [simply] said, 'a burnt-offering, a meal-offering'!" "Rather," said Rabba, "[this formulation] means that whoever occupies himself with the study of Torah needs neither burnt-offering nor meal-offering nor sin-offering nor guilt-offering." Rabbi Isaac said, "What is the significance of the verses 'This is the law of the sin-offering' [Leviticus 6:18] and 'This is the law of the guilt-offering' [7:1]? They teach that whoever is occupied with the laws of sin-offering is as if [*ke'ilu*] he were offering a sin-offering, and whoever is occupied with the laws of the guilt-offering is as if [ke'ilu] he were offering a guilt-offering."

The rhetorical cast of these interpretations should not gainsay their exhortatory force or, especially, the expiatory function of study proclaimed for Jews who lived after the destruction of the Temple and its service. Surely this reflects the ideals of the class of scholars who make these points; but just as surely does it betoken the changing notion of service ('avodah) which was then at work in Judaism. No longer the sacrificial service of the Shrine but now the devoted service of the heart (in prayer) and mind (in study) is proclaimed as the means of reparation between the individual and God. A more lapidary formulation found in b. Megillah 31b makes this point at the conclusion of a "dialogue" between God and Abraham. The latter asks how Israel can be protected from punishments due to sin when the Temple service does not exist, and is told: "I [God] have already established for them 'an order of sacrifices,' [so that] whenever they read from them I accredit [Israel] as if [ke'ilu] they make a sacrifice before Me – and I forgive all their sins." Other acts of substitution could also be included. Here we shall simply mention the poignant petition of Rav Sheshet, who, after a penitential fast, prayed "that my fat and blood which have diminished [through fasting] be as if [ke'ilu] I sacrificed them on the altar before You, and You favored me [with forgiveness]."[3] And then too there is the assertion that even if one brings only one's "self" (or "soul") before God in penitence, "it would be as if [ke'ilu] he sacrificed a soul."[4] We miss the living spirituality of these teachings if they are reduced to mere hyperbole. Imitative displacements of the sacrificial service (through fasting and penance and study) are all spiritual means to the same end. In this sense it is "as if" the worshipper were occupied with the Temple service itself.

Another group of sources may be added here: those dealing with the issue of the atoning power of suffering and individual death. This notion has ancient roots and extends by way of rabbinic literature into the Middle Ages, where it joins with rituals and attitudes bearing on our theme. Explicitly or implicitly, the repairing role of death or pain is always part of the ideational background, if only because they formed part of the curriculum which the scholars inherited and thus contributed to the folk ethos of those who absorbed such ideas from the liturgy, from sermons, or from common parlance. For our purposes, several formulations may be culled from the whole. Of these, two dicta mentioned in the Mishnah are striking, both for the ideas conveyed and for their liturgical significance. In the first, found in a discussion of the coloration of skin diseases, Rabbi Ishmael is reported to have said, "Children of Israel – I am their atonement!" That is, he accepted these sufferings *for the atonement* of the people. [5] In the second case, we learn that a person given a verdict of death by stoning is invited to confess just prior to reaching the place of execution; "but if he [the convict] does not know how to confess, they [the officials of the court] say to him: 'Say, "May my death atone for *all* my sins."'" [6] Both formulations attest to accepted theological values concerning atonement and provide legal support for their ritual pronouncement.

Both suffering and death as instruments of atonement are conjoined in an early list (together with repentance and the Day of Atonement) that considers various sins and their ritual remedies. [7] The capacity of the day of death to "cleanse" or "scrape away" sin is mentioned with respect to one who has "desecrated the Name of Heaven" [8] –

but only together with suffering (prior to death) and the appropriate acts of penitence. Among the biblical proof texts offered here is Isaiah 22:14, "Surely this sin shall not be atoned for [i.e., fully expiated] *until* you die." A dictum attributed to Rabbi Judah in the *Tosefta* gives a broader formulation: "Death and the Day of Atonement effect expiation together with repentance; repentance effects expiation along with death; and the day of death must be deemed like repentance."[9]

Classical Judaism thus struggled to assure the faithful that complete atonement for sins could be accomplished by the ritual and theological structures that remained after the loss of the sacrificial service. However apodictically formulated, one can easily sense the powerful impulses and anxieties that lie behind these teachings and the concern to base the outcome on biblically supported precedents. The notion that death is the ultimate sacrifice or expiatory act that can be offered for atonement provides great solace and influences Jewish attitudes both in the concrete act of sanctifying God in martyrdom and in the various ritual simulations (mental and physical) of death that developed in liturgical practice.

Before turning to the various forms of ritual simulation of death in Judaism (both mental and physical), it will be of interest to observe how the preceding traditions develop in the Middle Ages and combine to form the wider conceptual and theological framework of our specific theme. In this respect we may begin with Rav Sheshet's aforenoted prayer concerning the atoning power of one's "fat and blood" during penitential fasts. This theme recurs frequently in special synagogal prayers (*piyyuṭim*), particularly for Yom Kippur. Thus in a penitential prayer for that occasion, Levi ibn Altaban remarks how worshippers "offer their fat and blood / *like* sacrifices and burnt-offerings."[10] Rabbi Abraham ibn Ezra addresses God, "To You [O Lord] my heart and blood of my fat / I am *like* a lamb of burnt-offering."[11] Developing this theme, many medieval poets play on the alliteration of *dam* (blood) and *dem'a* (tear) and pray that God accept the gift of human tears as a sacrificial libation. In a particularly poignant stanza, Rabbi Shelomo ibn Gabirol intercedes for his people Israel (in a *rahiṭ* for Yom Kippur):

Lord! she has no [Temple] offering to atone for her guilt;
But her fat and blood replace the fat of peace-offerings,
And the sprinkling of her tears is *like* the sprinkling of her blood.
Sprinkle, then, O God, with Your healing waters and purify her![12]

We would seriously diminish the spiritual pathos of these prayers were we simply to relegate their sacrificial imagery to poetic tropes, to mere metaphors with no vital force. Rather, these petitions use ancient cultic terms to mediate and focus a concrete spiritual concern: divine atonement through vicarious sacrifice. Indeed, the penitents' desire for divine forgiveness is insistent throughout. For the sake of atonement, God is offered the flesh, blood, and tears of the penitent, even speech itself. In this last sense, the prayers have a confessional dimension and function like sacrificial offerings, in line with the dictum of the prophet Hosea, who urged his people to confess and say: "Instead of bulls we shall pay [the offering of] our lips" (14:3). Appreciating the force of this expression, an old talmudic tradition stresses the fact of substitution implied here and adds that one who confesses truly "is

regarded by Scripture as if [*ke'ilu*] he offered bulls [*parim*];
as it is written, 'Instead of bulls we shall pay [the offering
of] our lips'" (*b. Yoma* 86*b*). Annotating this teaching in
the eleventh century, Rabbeinu Ḥananel underscores the
point with the variant reading "as if he offered a sacrifice
[*qorban*]." The synagogue poets who were Ḥananel's near
and younger contemporaries wholeheartedly concurred
when they said, "Their [the penitents'] song [was] instead
of [*temur*] their offering [*qorbanam*].¹³

The spiritual power of prayer complements the other
(aforenoted) talmudic tradition regarding the study of the
rules of sacrifice. Indeed, the two themes conjoin in one
of the earliest works on halakhic practice: the *Sefer ha-
Manhig* of Rabbi Avraham ben Natan Hayarḥi of Lunel
(ca. 1155–1215). Referring to the requirement to recite
the rules of daily sacrifices (*parashat temidin*) every day,
the author adds: "and these are accounted before God in
place of an offering [*u-bimqom qorban hen neḥeshavim lifnei
ha-maqom*]; as it is stated: 'We shall pay the fruit [*peri!*] of
our lips.'"¹⁴ Following this Sefardi tradition, Abudarham
(fourteenth century) states that the rabbis ruled regarding
the recitation of "the sacrifices more than other topics
since whoever recites these with intention [*kavanat ha-
lev*], it is as if [*ke'ilu*] he offered them [in sacrifice]."¹⁵
The concern was also well-established in the Ashkenazi
rite. Thus by the thirteenth century, Rabbi Zedekiah ben
Avraham Ha-Rofe (of Italy) refers to the daily recitation
of the *tamid*-sacrifice in his *Shibbolei ha-Leqeṭ* as something
"required" (*ve-tzarikh . . . liqrot*);¹⁶ and the saintly Rabbi
Eleazar ben Rabbi Yehuda (of Worms) commented on the
words "to sacrifice to Me" in the *tamid*-service, saying:
"The *tamid* should always be performed; and if one should
object and say that it is [now] annulled [because of the
Temple's destruction], one may answer this [with the

Ritual Simulation and Substitution

biblical verse] 'Instead of bulls we shall pay [the offering of] our lips' and [with the rabbinical dictum] 'Prayer has been established in lieu of sacrifices.'"[17]

Gradually, statements stressing the substitution of verbal recitation for sacrifices were incorporated into the prayer book and became an explicit petition interleaved with the paragraphs recounting the actual sacrifices. Thus by the sixteenth century, Rabbi Moshe ibn Makhir (of Safed) notes that after reciting the *tamid*-sacrifice the worshipper says, "May the words of our lips be deemed worthy and acceptable as if [*ke'ilu*] we offered the *tamid*-sacrifice at its appointed time." Similarly, Rabbi Yosef Karo ruled that after the sacrificial recitations (concluding with *parashat ha-'olah*), one should say: "May it be Your will that this be deemed worthy and acceptable as if [*ke'ilu*] I offered the *'olah*-sacrifice."[18] These phrases recur in the Ashkenazi rite, along with a more explicit account of the atoning purpose of this prayer. Thus, just before reciting the rules of sacrifice, one is bidden to add:

May it be Your will, O Lord our God and God of our ancestors, that You have mercy upon us and forgive all our sins and grant us atonement for all our iniquities and wipe away all our transgressions; and that You build the Temple speedily in our day that we may offer to You the daily [*tamid*] sacrifice, that it provide atonement for us . . .

A third aspect of ritual simulation returns us to the theme of *kiddush ha-shem,* or martyrdom, discussed in the previous chapter. We there had occasion to observe that Rabbi Yosef Yuzpe Hahn (in the seventeenth century) invoked Rabbi Eliezer Azikri with respect to his teaching that if one did not have the opportunity to die a martyr in fact, then a sincere mental intention could suffice.

Ritual Simulation and Substitution

For this spiritual substitution to be effective, however, the worshipper must be utterly resolved (*gamar be-libbo*) to die a martyr. As noted, the purpose of this ritual replacement was to enable the devotee to fulfill *all* the commandments of the Torah, and thus achieve absolute perfection (and with it release from the round of rebirth). The Kabbalistic theosophy underpinning this concern for ritual perfection was clearly articulated by Rabbi Yosef Hahn's contemporary Rabbi Isaiah Horowitz of Prague. In his masterwork, the *Shnei Lukhot ha-Berit,* Rabbi Isaiah Horowitz noted the mystical tradition that each of the 613 commandments of Jewish observance is related to a different part of the Supernal Anthropos, a spiritual structure in the highest realm which is also the archetype for the human anthropoidal configuration on earth. Accordingly, one of the mysteries of the commandments performed by mortals is the simultaneous capacity of these acts to repair (and rebuild) the heavenly form while perfecting the earthly self.[19] Individual and cosmic eschatology are thus interdependent, and absolutely dependent upon the human performance of every divine law – even those that are physically precluded by spatial setting (e.g., not living in the land of Israel), historical occasion (e.g., martyrdom), or social events (e.g., levirite marriage or writing a bill of divorce). So what can one do under such circumstances? Developing an older solution, Rabbi Isaiah Horowitz offers a profound reinterpretation of the ancient ideal of study for its own sake and combines it with the notion of "spiritual preparation" (*hakhanah*).[20]

The SHeLaH (as Horowitz was called, after the acronym from the title of his book) begins with the old problem of how the ancient Patriarchs achieved spiritual perfection, since they lived before Sinai and thus did not have the concrete commandments to perform. His answer is that they realized the commandments in a wholly interior way, through "the power of their preparation [*hakhanatam*]; that is, they were absolutely attached [*devuqim be-takhlit ha-devequt*] to the Creator, may He be blessed, and were joyfully prepared [*mukhanim*] to fulfill His will in whatever He might command them. . . . And this preparation [*hakhanah*] was *like* the actual deed [*ke-ma'aseh be-fo'al*]." What is more, through the strength of their "absolute preparation" (*takhlit ha-hakhanah*), these saints realized the entirety of 613 commandments through the commandments they did perform, for the totality was "included" [*kelulim*] in each and every *mitzvah*. After Sinai, however, when the 613 commandments were revealed, pious people practiced what they could do in fact (*be-fo'al*) and remained prepared to fulfill all of them joyously, so that "what one cannot fulfill [in fact] is '[accounted] as if [*ke'ilu*] he [actually] fulfilled [it], since he is prepared [to do so]" through study of the Torah for its own sake. "Thus even though one may not fulfill [a commandment] because it is unavailable to him to do so, but he is [nevertheless] prepared [*mukhan*] to fulfill it, then [the commandment] is accounted to such a one as if [*ke'ilu*] he fulfilled it – because he brought the deed to actuality by the power of this preparation [*hakhanah*]."

For Rabbi Isaiah Horowitz, the public revelation of all the commandments is deemed a special theological moment, effected by God for "the generation which proved worthy" – though there is a noticeable shift from the exalted spiritual preparation of the Patriarchs, which was linked to their absolute *devequt* (attachment), to a preparation expressed through pure study. Although the latter "performance" of the commandments is deemed effective and demands great spiritual development, it is noteworthy that the language of *devequt* is not used in connection with it. Perhaps for this reason Rabbi Isaiah Horowitz's son, Rabbi Shabbetai Sheftel, sensed a diminution in spiritual capacity from the Patriarchs to the generation of Sinai and somewhat undermines his father's point when he comments that the Israelites at Sinai needed a multitude of commandments in order to achieve divine merit, because their preparation was not as strong as that of their ancestors. In a striking reversal, Rabbi Shabbetai Sheftel goes on to close the gap opened by his father's omission when he says that the people's "preparation" (*hakhanatam*) is "the attachment [*devequt*] to God, may He be praised, within them."[21]

The SHeLaH refers to the capacity of the individual to fulfill the commandments through mental preparation as "a very great mystery" (*rav hu sod ha-hakhanah*) and invokes the ancient rabbinic dictum that "whoever occupies himself with the portion of sacrifices is [accounted] as if [*ke'ilu*] he offered the sacrifices [themselves]" (*b. Menaḥot* 110a). The emphasis here remains on personal perfection. Elsewhere, the author returns to this teaching in the context of considering how the Temple service can be actualized in the present day (*ha'idana*), now that the Temple is in ruins. The perspective thus shifts to a broader, sacramental dimension as three levels of sacrificial simulation are recorded. In ancient days, when the Temple still stood, a person could worship God correctly through action, word, and thought: through (the act of) sacrifice, the (recitation of the) confession, and the (focused) articulation of the divine Name. But now:

A person must offer himself [sacrificially; *yaqriv 'et 'atzmo*] in action. [And] how [does he do] so? By means of [abject] mourning for Jerusalem, which he demonstrates through all his actions. . . .

Ritual Simulation and Substitution

[And he must offer himself] in word. How so? [By means of the principle] "Instead of bulls we shall pay [the offering of] our lips"; as our sages of blessed memory have said: "Whoever occupies himself with the portion of the sacrifices is as if he offered the sacrifices [themselves]."

[And he must also offer himself] in thought. How so? [This he does through] the mystery [whereby] one determines in his mind [*gamar be-libbo*] to devote himself to the sanctification of the Name; for then he fulfills in himself [the verse] "A person who would offer from among you [a sacrifice to YHWH]" [Leviticus 1:2], since he offers himself [sacrificially] to God, may He be praised. [And as regards the continuity of the verse], "If his offering is from the sheep," [this may be understood] with regard to [the martyrologically understood passage] "we are regarded as sheep for the slaughter."[22]

In this passage we have an interesting sequence of simulations from the physical to the verbal to the mental (i.e., intentional), all focused on Temple piety, with three eschatological effects: the *national* rebuilding of the Temple (through absolute mourning, as the passage itself says), the *personal* perfection of the self (through atonement for all sins), and the sanctification of the *divine* (through readiness for martyrdom). This last sanctification is more literally the sanctification of the divine Name, as we have seen earlier, and so it may be fitting to conclude this initial synopsis of ritual simulations with another passage from the *SHeLaH* which integrates action, speech, and thought on a spiritual level. This is a prayer for the reparation (*tikkun*) of the divine Name and is by any measure a remarkable expression of the attitude toward ritual reality we have been tracing. In it the speaker seeks to restore the defects caused through sin to each of the four letters of the divine Name, or to the other letters of the alphabet mystically connected to it.[23] Moving from the first to the fourth letter of the Tetragrammaton, the supplicant intends to repair each of the four hierarchical worlds (in descending series) dependent upon them through his acknowledgment that each one requires death by one of the four types of capital punishment (stoning, burning, decapitation, and strangulation) prescribed by the ancient rabbinical court. At each of the first three stages the speaker further invokes the intercessory merit of the Patriarchs, and at all four points he declares himself as (ke'ilu) one killed by the court in the proper way. Though simulated, such deaths effect nothing less than a *tikkun,* or atoning reparation, for the supernal divine reality. In the summarizing finale, intention and recitation are brought to a striking close when the worshipper beseeches God to give him the strength to undertake these sufferings with a pure mind and pure speech. With paradoxical poignancy, the divine is perfected through power bestowed upon the "dying" human sinner. Quite different features of simulated death will occupy us in subsequent pages.

In the previous chapter, the striking testimony of Rabbi Abraham ben Eliezer Halevi was adduced with respect to a person who truly "determines" (*gomer be-libbo*) to sacrifice himself for the honor of God. Such a person, he remarked, does not feel the tortures brought upon him. He had this as "a tradition among the sages"; and we find one source in the thirteenth-century responsum of Rabbi Meir of Rothenberg, who notes this capacity to transcend pain when a person fully "determines" (*gomer be-da'ato*) to die a faithful martyr.[24] A similar expression to indicate spiritual intent is found in a contemporary (thirteenth-century) Spanish commentary on the commandments by Rabbi Moshe de Leon, the *Sefer ha-Rimmon.* The important

Ritual Simulation and Substitution

difference for our purposes lies in the fact that the author is concerned to instruct his readers in the proper intentions to keep in mind while reciting the Shema (Deuteronomy 6:4–6) in the daily liturgy. Referring to the mishnaic and midrashic understanding of the phrase "with all your soul" as meaning "even if He takes your soul," de Leon cites the following (earlier) tradition:

Every person who loves his Creator, whenever he reaches the verse "and you shall love (etc.)" in the recitation of the Shema, should direct his mind and thoughts toward love for his Maker, as if [ke'ilu] he were giving up his soul for His sake in love, with absolute sincerity, and accepting death upon himself. And it is obligatory upon each person to resolve [lit., "determine"; *ligmor be-nafsho*] this matter daily. And this is like what [the sages meant when] they said, "For Your sake we are killed all day long, and regarded as sheep for the slaughter." And how splendid if he employs this intention daily in love for his Maker and devotes his soul for His sake, as we have said; and He, may He be blessed, wants intention [in worship].[25]

Here we have a spiritual intention concerning martyrological devotion during prayer, long before the supposed shift from acts of concrete performance (during the Crusades) to their ritual enactment (during the sixteenth to eighteenth centuries).[26] What is more, this valuable document already employs the word *ke'ilu* to mark the meditative act involved. In contrast to contemporary and later uses of the "as if" formula to indicate projective visualizations of the divine Name (and other matters),[27] de Leon counsels a mental focusing of intent – a projection of will – performed daily. The goal is thus to enact the commitment to die as an expression of absolute loving devotion. And although nothing further is said here regarding actual martyrological practice, it is clear from de Leon's theosophical introduction that such a "death-act" has practical benefits. In the first place, he remarks that the commitment of human love is a pillar that sustains the universe,[28] even as it is a means of restoring one's divine nature to its transcendental source.[29] And finally, drawing on a discussion of the capacity of joyful service to draw forth heavenly blessing from the supernal gradations (of divine Being), de Leon speaks of the "holy martyrs," who "accepted death in love, through the mystery of joy." While cleaving to God in love, supernal Joy descended upon them; so that "they were joyful in their sufferings"![30] Alluding to Rabbi Akiba's celebrated theology of "the sufferings of love" (*b. Berakhot 5a*), the text invokes the model of Akiba, who accepted his torturous death with a resolute spirit, and who, because of his great attachment to God while reciting the Shema at his death, *"did not feel his torture!"* Intense love may thus lead to the transcendence of pain, as Rabbi Meir of Rothenberg and Rabbi Abraham ben Eliezer attested, and as de Leon himself seems wont to counsel his compatriots. The proper practice of the daily Shema is then as much a preparation for saintly death as it is a credo of living love of God. The ritual recitation is thus an interiorization of death, such that the true devotee is already in life a spiritual martyr in deed.

This interpretation of the Shema recitation as a meditation on martyrological death recurs throughout the Middle Ages – and beyond. Particularly influential was the annotation of the celebrated sixteenth-century talmudist Rabbi Joel Sirkis to Rabbi Jacob ben Asher's monumental code, the *Arba'ah Ṭurim*.

When one recites the Shema, one should have the intention to accept upon oneself the yoke of the Kingdom of Heaven,

Ritual Simulation and Substitution

to be slain for the sanctification of the Name. . . . This is what is meant by "with all your soul" – even if He takes your soul. . . . With this intention one will recite it with fear and trembling.[31]

The issue comes up in other sixteenth-century documents and genres. Thus Rabbi Eliezer Azikri counsels in his spiritual compendium *Sefer Ḥaredim* that one should resolutely intend to die a martyr while reciting the Shema, so that if the event should come to pass, he would devote himself to God "in joy." This prayerful resolution "would be accounted [*neḥeshav*] to him as if [*ke'ilu*] he devoted himself in fact."[32] Such a point, it will be recalled, was made by Rabbi Yosef Hahn (who also alludes to Azikri's manual) in the next century, and it achieved a summary formulation by the eighteenth-century Kabbalist and moralist Rabbi Moshe Ḥayyim Luzzatto, in his spiritual guidebook *Derekh ha-Shem*:

One of the conditions associated with this commandment [of reciting the Shema] is that each person mentally resolve [*gomer be-da'ato*] to devote his soul for the sake of God's Unity and willingly undergo all manner of sufferings and types of death for the sanctification of His Name – and [such a resolve] will be accounted [*neḥeshav*] as if [*ke'ilu*] he did the deed in fact and was slain for the sanctification of the Name. [Such a resolve,] moreover, has great consequences for the benefit of the Creation and the more general rectification. (IV.4.iv)

Several matters are intertwined here. Beginning with the traditional emphasis on the meritorious benefits accruing to the individual worshipper who determines to die a martyr while reciting the Shema, the passage ends with a reference to the greater boon befalling Creation and the overall redemption. Indeed, the meditative act not only produces a ritual exchange of thought for divine merit but has a theurgical effect on the fragments of fallen existence awaiting rectification. Put differently, but in the linguistic spirit of Luzzatto's formulation, the intense human resolve to sacrifice oneself for divine Unity actually influences the restorative unification of all Being. Self-sacrifice thus stands in the center of world-restorative actions, actually replacing the ancient Temple as the site of ritual at-one-ment. In this regard, the allusion to the old rabbinic list of effective expiations (mentioned earlier) cannot be overlooked. According to both the *Mekhilta de-Rabbi Ishmael* and the *Tosefta*,[33] desecration of the divine Name requires (along with repentance and the Day of Atonement) suffering and death itself. Now, as if in response, Luzzatto says that the mental resolve to suffer and die for the sanctification of God's Name is not only like the real occurrence of such actions but even actualizes cosmic dimensions as well. Verbal proclamation and mental resolve thus combine as two sides of a performative utterance – with divine effect.

Integrating a martyrological "configuration" into one's imagination is one way that a simulation of death-in-love was enacted in Jewish ritual. A more physical procedure is the penitential practice of *nefilat 'appayim*, a simulated prostration performed in the morning and afternoon daily service, immediately after the public repetition of the Amidah prayer, the central standing prayer of the liturgy.[34] Depending upon customary procedure, the worshipper either first recites a confession and the thirteen attributes of divine mercy or immediately enacts the prostration rite and recites a psalm. In ancient rabbinic times, according to talmudic tradition (cf. *b. Megillah*

Ritual Simulation and Substitution

22a), it was customary for one to actually lie prostrate and request divine mercy. This abject act of humility and self-nullification was commuted to the more symbolic gesture of leaning to one side while seated: to the right side in the morning (because the phylacteries are worn on the left arm) and to the left in the afternoon, according to Ashkenazi custom.[35] At this point, either Psalm 6 (in the Ashkenazi rite) or 25 (in the Sephardi and Kabbalistic rite) is recited.[36] On Mondays and Thursdays the Ve-Hu Raḥum penitential is added as well.

Various explanations for the *nefilat 'appayim* rite are found in the sources. They reflect different spiritual dimensions and concerns, as well as various modes of self-nullification and death enactment. To appreciate the spectrum of moral and mythic interpretations, and the psychological or theosophical poles of the rite, we shall begin with the fairly straightforward commentary of Rabbeinu Baḥye ben Asher (thirteenth century) on Numbers 16:22 and conclude with examples a half-millennium later dealing with mystical death and the kiss of God. A window is thereby opened to the rich inner world of Jewish liturgical practice and, in particular, to one of its most intriguing gestures.

Following the rebellion of Korah and his cohorts in the wilderness (Numbers 16), God tells Moses and Aaron to separate themselves from the sinning congregation that He might destroy the rebels. The two men thereupon fall upon their faces (*va-yiplu 'al peneihem*) in order to supplicate divine mercy. On the phrase "they fell upon their faces" (v. 22), Baḥye comments:

To pray. And from [this passage we derive the act of] *nefilat 'appayim* in prayer. And know that the matter of *nefilat 'appayim* in prayer has three purposes. The first is [to express] the fear of the divine Presence; the second is to demonstrate sadness and submission; and the third is to show the restraint of sensations and the nullification of feelings. [As regards] the first, [which deals with] the fear of the divine Presence, [the rite helps one] express shame and humility, since the covering of [one's] face [in the rite] is a form of humility and shamefacedness. . . . The second [purpose], to demonstrate sadness and submission, is that one who falls upon his face is sorrowful and submissive – and submission is of the essence of repentance, such that God senses the regret of the worshipper and fulfills his request. . . . [And] the third [purpose], to demonstrate the restraint of sensations and the nullification of feelings, is because one who falls upon his face, covers his face, and closes his mouth concurs that he does not know his [fate] . . . , and [acts] as if his feelings are nullified and restrained from his desires. And as regards his [closed] eyes and sealed mouth, [these symbolize] that he is unable to see or speak other than what expresses the will of God, be He blessed.[37]

Most striking is the religious psychology conveyed here. Speaking as a pedagogue and pietist, Rabbeinu Baḥye seeks to explain the custom of prostration in prayer in terms of a symbolic language that speaks to God of the worshipper's spiritual intentions: his abject humility before God's majesty, his total remorse before God's providence, and his ascetic control before earthly desire and God's will. The body, face, mouth, and eyes are all part of a syntax of piety that trains the worshipper in the values of humility, even as they simultaneously bespeak the incorporation of these values. Located just after the supplications which conclude the Amidah prayer, the ritual of *nefilat 'appayim* enacts the utter dependence of the individual upon God for all favors and the resolve to be a submissive servant to Him. The emotion of shame is therefore central. By means of the rite, pride is laid low and the self grounded in religious humility.

Perceived theologically, the issue of shame is part of the self's internal response to the divine Presence and evokes (in the ideal scenario) the repentant self-transformation of the worshipper. In this and related formulations, such a dynamic is often the way medieval Jewish thinkers construct the relationship between the renewal of religious sensibility in fear or awe of God and its eventual supplementation by covenantal love and faith. I mention this because it helps highlight the interesting difference between Baḥye's discussion and the contemporary mythic theosophy portrayed in the *Zohar*. In one passage, the recitation of the Amidah brings about a conjunction of the masculine and feminine dimensions of God. "In shame" before this cosmic coupling, the worshipper falls forward and covers his face while focusing his mind on the birth of souls resulting from this Holy Union (II.128b–129a). The purpose of this physical and mental exercise is to undergo a cycle of death and rebirth, insofar as the worshipper "devotes his soul" to the feminine dimension. By thus cleaving to Her when She is "taking" souls, the worshipper is born anew (II.200b).[38] Accordingly, the expression of shame in this scenario induces a spiritual (rather than psychological) transformation of the worshipper; a change that results from cleaving to the divine during its process of regeneration.

In other cases, it is precisely the readiness or resolve to die during the rite of *nefilat 'appayim* that is decisive for the worshipper; that is, the penitent physically expresses the intention to die at the hands of the Shekhinah, the feminine aspect of God, who is symbolized by the Tree of Death. The process is as follows. During the upright Amidah prayer the mystically minded person is supposed to be

physically attached to the masculine principle known as
Tiferet, the vertical column of the divine hierarchy that
helps link the upper feminine grade with the lower one
(*Malkhut;* i.e., the Shekhinah).[39] This masculine aspect
is also symbolized by the Tree of Life. Accordingly,
when the worshipper detaches his meditative attention
from *Tiferet* at the conclusion of the Amidah, he must
immediately acknowledge the feminine side of Death,
that he not die altogether. "It is thus necessary for a person
– immediately upon concluding the Amidah – to regard
himself as if [*ke'ilu*] he departed from the world" (III.120*b*).
This is done through the mimetic act of *nifilat 'appayim,*
whereby he falls face forward and (through reciting Psalm
25) redeposits his soul with the same feminine aspect of
God with which he deposits it at night – but now not in a
temporary way "but as one who actually [*vada'i*] departs
from the world" (III.121*a*).

Functioning at several levels, this ritual process is at once
an integration (within the worshipper) of the opposites of
life and death, a unification (for God's sake) of the Trees
of Life and Death, and a human attachment to the divine
Tree of Death for the sake of renewed life. The last point
is vital, for as the *Zohar* states, "The secret [i.e., mystical]
explanation [of this rite] is that there are sins which remain
unatoned for until a person departs from the world, as is
said, 'This sin will not be expiated until you die' [Isaiah
22:14]. Thus [the worshipper] should give himself truly
over to death and devote his soul to that [other] 'place' –
not as a [temporary] deposit [of the soul] as [done] at night
but as if he actually [*vada'i*] departed from this world."[40]
Absolute sincerity is thus essential for this atonement to
"work"; no dissembling of death is allowed. The absence
of the letter vav (numerically, 6) from the acrostic in Psalm
25 is said to hint at this as well, since the principle of

Ritual Simulation and Substitution

"Life" and the gradations of *Tiferet* are symbolized by this letter (and number), and the worshipper must abandon these for "Death" after the Amidah prayer (III.121*b*). Moreover, the letter quf is missing as well – to teach that the worshipper should not dissemble death like the (proverbial) monkey (*qof*) who pretended to be dead when a serpent (*ḥivta'*, which is a pun on "life" and is symbolic of the Shekhinah) came to kill it. Only loving sincerity ensures divine favor and the forgiveness of sins.[41] In his Hebrew work *Sefer ha-Rimmon,* de Leon mentions these missing letters but demythologizes the explanation and neutralizes the zoharic notion of succumbing to the dark side of "Death."[42]

In some of the previous texts, the *Zohar* employs a double locution to indicate the status of the ritual action performed. On the one hand, the death simulation is marked by the term *ke'ilu.* This serves notice that the ritual is merely "like" the death of the worshipper; it is only "as if" the performer died in the rite. On the other hand, the action is termed *vada'i;* that is, something "actual" – a veritable deed, "indeed." At the semantic level, such a combination of verisimilitude and actuality is an oxymoron. But as ritual denotations, this paradox finely expresses the double dimension of ritual performance: mimetic substitutes for actions "in the world" are believed to effect changes in this or otherworldly realms, "as if" those (conscious) imitations were the real thing. Accordingly, it is not necessary to die in fact in order to receive the benefits of death (like expiation); and to be reborn to life on a higher spiritual plane, one must merely (i.e., *actually* – in the ritual) be "as if" dead while the heavenly conjunctions are occurring. Action alone, however, does not suffice. Also required are the proper

Ritual Simulation and Substitution

mental intention and the requisite verbal recitation. In the cases discussed, these include the decision to consider oneself dead and the recitation of Psalm 25 ("To You, O Lord, I deliver my soul!" v. 1). Action, speech, and thought thus form a triple cord of ritual efficacy. It is the well-tempered concordance of gesture, word, and intention that makes the rite work.

Subsequent Kabbalistic tradition developed one or another feature of the zoharic myths associated with *nefilat 'appayim* and gave the performer new powers and tasks. An interesting (and influential) conspectus is found in the commentary on the standard prayers by Rabbi Moshe Cordovero (1522–70) – the preeminent Kabbalist in Safed before Rabbi Yitzḥaq Luria, and his teacher. In his *Tefillah le-Moshe,* some old and new features are mentioned.[43] Thus, in one context he quotes a long citation from the *Zohar* (III.120b–121a) dealing with the atonement that death brings and draws several conclusions.[44] The first is a mere paraphrase of the point that one should consider oneself during the rite "as if" one had departed this world; but Cordovero also notes that this (death–offering) is "to appease" the Creator, even if one achieves only a brief ascension into "the exalted union" (*be-yiḥud ha-'elyon*). This consideration not only underscores the symbolic sacrifice of the rite but indicates that this deposit of the soul on high is a cleaving of the soul to the Godhead. This is probably not a mystical conjunction so much as an intense concentration upon supernal realities. The *Zohar* itself mentions as much when it says that this "reparation" for the soul requires *kavvanah de-libba'* (spiritual intention) and that one is required "to cause his soul and will to cleave to his Lord" without guile.

After this Cordovero shifts planes and indicates the higher purpose of this personal sacrifice and its effect on the divine world. First, he says, this symbolic death is "for the sake" of the feminine gradation of Divinity (*Malkhut*), because the principle of Death adheres to Her (as we have noted); and then, too, one should "die" so as to purge Her of the "defect" caused by acts of desecration of the Name, because only death expiates such disruption of the divine harmony. By this atoning act, the female *Malkhut* is able "to unite with Her beloved [*Tiferet*]." An act of human conjunction (*yiḥud*) thus helps effect a supernal union (*tityaḥḥed*) within the Godhead. Furthermore, the aspect of the "reparation" of the human body in the rite also enacts the conjunction (and thus reparation) on high; for Cordovero goes on to say that the worshipper should perform *nifilat 'appayim* by leaning to the left (the Sefardi and Kabbalistic custom) and "grasping it [*leḥabbeqah;* i.e., the left arm] with the right [hand] to indicate that the intention [of the ritual] is that She [*Malkhut*] be joined and embraced [*le-ḥabbeqah*] on high between the arms of the King [*Tiferet*]; . . . and that is [like what is written in Songs 2:6]: 'His left [arm] is beneath my head, and His right embraces me [*tiḥabbeqeini*].'"

At this point, the ancient rite of *nefilat 'appayim* is not only (as in the zoharic traditions) a penitential act of humility or inner transformation; and it is even more than an act effecting expiation for defects in the upper and lower spheres. By virtue of the enactment of Songs 2:6, interpreted as a conjunction of the masculine and feminine aspects of divinity, the worshipper physically imitates this supernal syzygy while intending it in his mind. The person thus becomes aligned with the masculine King, *Tiferet,* who is aroused to union with His beloved, who has been purged of desecrations brought about by human sin. However, this is not all. Immediately following this point, Cordovero says that in the process of binding

Ritual Simulation and Substitution

Malkhut to *Tiferet* on high, "he [the worshipper] becomes the Female Waters [*mayyin nuqvin*]"; that is, the fertilizing fluids that prepare *Malkhut* to receive the downward thrust of heavenly blessings, which may, through her, inseminate the earthly realm.[45] We are thus faced with a true mystery rite of transformation whereby the worshipper is *simultaneously* both the heavenly Male and the heavenly Female. As Life and Death are integrated within him, so are they integrated on high. Indeed, through a symbolic death the penitent is now an agent of cosmic regeneration – even rebirth, for the reunited Bride and Bridegroom may now ascend to the supernal womb of the Mother (*'Imma'; the gradation of *Binah*), in which they were formed.[46]

The mythic aspects of Cordovero's interpretations of the *nefilat 'appayim* rite are bold and daring but relatively underdeveloped as compared with those of his disciple Rabbi Yitzḥaq Luria Ashkenazi ("the sainted ARI").[47] In his view, the worshipper (in an ideal sense, for the task requires consummate skill and is filled with spiritual danger) performs heroic exploits in the cosmic realms – releasing souls trapped in the husks of Gehenna and bearing them aloft through the four divine worlds, where they help accomplish a conjunction of masculine and feminine elements in the supernal spheres.[48] As a result of the holy prayers of Israel, these souls are purged and transformed into *mayyin nuqvin*, which the worshipper collects and raises to the (masculine) gradation of *Ze'ir 'Anpin* in the highest world (*'Atzilut;* Emanation).[49] It is here that drops of mercy have secreted from higher aspects of this anthropomorphic configuration, as a result of the previous recitation of prayers in the liturgy. They now enter the generative principle of *Ze'ir 'Anpin,* which is "Jacob," who unites with "Rachel," his beloved.

Ritual Simulation and Substitution

Remarkably, all this is achieved through a consummate act of spiritual intention, as the worshipper first imagines himself physically hurled from the exalted world of *'Atzilut* (which he has attained through the Amidah prayer, just concluded) to the nethermost realm, *'Aśiyah* (the world of Making), and then concentrates upon his ascension with the transfigured souls. The act of *nefilat 'appayim* is thus conceived here as a real fall into the divine abyss, and as such is fraught with danger. Luria therefore cautions his reader not to attempt these feats unless he is truly righteous and can withstand contact with evil. There are those who barely escape with their own souls intact. Others never ascend; such souls are transfigured by their own acts of imagination and remain in this dimension or "world."[50] In these cases the shamanic descent is aborted, and an act of salvation ends in spiritual suicide.

In the course of other elaborations of the worshipper's journey, Luria speculates that the redemptive goal is for the adept to join the three aspects of his soul (life force, spirit, supersoul) to the corresponding aspects of lost souls in each of the three lower worlds, and thence to raise them to the gradation of *Ze'ir 'Anpin* in the fourth world through the mystery of the *mayyin nuqvin*. In a more complex alternative, the performer of the *nefilat 'appayim* rite is bidden to take only the soul aspect called life force from the fivefold configuration of souls in each of the three lower worlds – each ensemble of five being labeled with one of the three main terms for soul.[51] Such arcana mark the perilous rescue of entrapped fragments of divinity which the worshipper intends to redeem for the sake of the Godhead itself. As an act of devotion of the self (*mesirat nefesh*), it borders on the spectacular; but it is not the spectacular itself. This exalted position is reserved for devotion unto death in the course of reciting the Shema in the (twice) daily liturgy or during the (unique) act of martyrological sanctification of the Name. Luria thus conceives a hierarchy of death devotions that dominate the intentions and imagination of the Jew at prayer.[52]

Of the two main types of *mesirat nefesh* unto death, the ritual of *nefilat 'appayim* is the type performed by the righteous, who in their reparation of souls activate a syzygy in the lower reaches of the Godhead (*Tiferet* and *Malkhut*) in the highest world, setting in motion a well of saving waters that flow upward from the feminine (the womb of the righteous in heaven) and downward from the masculine gradation. This temporary conjunction is the result of the enacted death of the worshipper, who is "*as if* departed from the world." Its liturgical rubric is "To You [*'eleykha*], O Lord, I deliver my soul" (Psalm 25:1); that is, the adept only raises his soul to the hypostatic gradation of "Lord" (the masculine dimension of *Tiferet*) – no further.[53] By contrast, through the martyrological intention of the Shema recitation in the liturgy, the worshipper activates a higher syzygy (the supernal Father and Mother, *Hokhmah* and *Binah*); for he now intends to die in fact and, in accord with the key verse "For Your sake [*'aleykha*] we are killed all day long" (Psalm 44:23), actually goes "to the One who is above You" (*'aleykha;* i.e., to *Hokhmah,* who is above *Tiferet*).[54] This produces a more permanent union in the supernal realm – all the more so when the recitation of the Shema accompanies an actual martyrdom.

This was the effect of Rabbi Akiba's death, when, in an ecstatic moment, he passed beyond Moses (in *Tiferet*) and ascended (*'alah*) to the gradation of *Hokhmah*, also called *Mahashavah* (Thought). In this way, Luria transforms God's answer to Moses in the rabbinic legend of Akiba's death. As discussed earlier,[55] Moses complained

Ritual Simulation and Substitution

that Akiba's torture made a mockery of piety; but he was caught short by the divine remark, "Thus have I determined" (lit., "[for] so has it arisen in [My] thought"). In one stroke this brusque theodicy is transformed, and Moses (the righteous prophet) who died by a divine kiss is superseded in the heavenly realms by Akiba (the sainted martyr), who ascended to the highest gradation of the Godhead (the pinnacle of Thought in the Mind of the Heavenly Anthropos that constitutes the highest world; thus, the divine comment was exegetically construed to mean "[for] so has he [Akiba] ascended into [the supernal sphere of] Thought"!). It may be that this transcendental ascension influenced the author of 'Arvei Naḥal centuries later, when he used just this rabbinic episode to say that saints may overcome the pains of martyrdom if they truly cleave to God in their last trial.[56]

There thus transpires in Luria's scheme a hierarchy of kisses (nishiqin) in the divine realm brought about by different levels of loving devotion (mesirat nefesh) unto death. Moving upward, the following spectrum may be delineated. In the (relatively) lower reaches of the Godhead (for we are dealing with transformations in the divine structure in 'Atzilut, the highest world), there is "the mystery of the lower kisses" – a syzygy effected between Tiferet and Malkhut by those individuals who either intend upon a martyr's death in the course of the liturgy or have this in mind at the moment of their (natural) death. The first is a symbolic exchange of human death for renewed life in the divine Being (the one activates the other); the second is "the mystery of the death of the righteous by a kiss," which now means that when the righteous die, there is a heavenly conjunction that releases Life and Blessing to the world. The blissful death of the righteous is thus an earthly figure of a transcendental state:

grace below activates Grace above; the perfected soul of the righteous is a sacrificial sacrament, so to speak, that "inspires" divine Life.[57]

The highest conjunction of divine qualities occurs between the supernal gradations of Ḥokhmah and Binah (Wisdom and Understanding) and is referred to as "the mystery of the supernal kisses." This syzygy is assisted by Moses through "the mystery of Knowledge" and by those (like Akiba) who devote themselves to death for the sanctification of the divine Name. The theosophical role of Moses is thus double: having reached the gradation of Tiferet he generates a unification in the lower Godhead; and in that very station he is in a position to serve as a "chariot" (or armature) for the higher and more interior unification of Ḥokhmah and Binah. But for our theme, the role of Akiba and the martyrs in the divine economy is more astonishing; for the blood and devotion of these saints not only repair disjunctions in the divine Being but activate a supernal bliss that overflows into all realms of existence. It is thus not just the mystery of death that stands at the heart of All-Being but the sacrificial death of humans that mysteriously redeems the Godhead. The hierarchy (and variety) of deathlike intentions in the liturgy thus reaches its apex in the loving death of martyrs for God's Name (whose various formulations – the Tetragrammaton YHWH in Tiferet and the revelatory 'eHYeH, "I shall Be," in the hidden heights – are therewith unified).[58] Mythic sacrifice does not then generate the diffusion and even fracturing of Being in the preternatural and primordial times of Beginning; but it does, in the form of mystical devotion of self, regenerate holy hierarchies and restore harmony to the divine Whole. Death is the paradoxical agent of Life: a salvific-messianic act with human love at the center.

Ritual Simulation and Substitution

In the system of Rabbi Yitzḥaq Luria, the rituals of *nefilat 'appayim* and Shema recitation are two types of devotion of the self focused on theosophical realities; and the explicit emphasis is on mystical intentions that effect changes in Divinity. Inwardness or even ecstatic states are not mentioned except to indicate the requisite meditative focus that may produce the desired ends. However, one of the well-known features of the revival of Hasidic piety in the eighteenth century is a concerted shift of emphasis away from the theosophy of divine attributes toward their psychologization in the "inner world" of the individual. At one level, this cultivation of a theological anthropology is merely (though significantly) the elaborated application of the old dogma that humans are created in the image of God. But on another level it opened new spaces in the spiritual life of the worshipper and provided maps for exploring mystical states and self-perfection. The remarkable tract on ecstasy, called *Qunṭeres ha-Hitpa'alut,* by Rabbi Dov Ber (son of Rabbi Shneur Zalman of Liadi) reveals this development in highly calibrated formulations.[59] A column of (natural and divine) souls and soul states is the axis along which a devotee may ascend to exalted levels of mystical expiry. Not unexpectedly, Dov Ber emphasizes the ecstatic possibilities available through recital of the Shema.[60] Properly performed, this prayer can enable the adept to reach a level of ecstasy in which the contemplative mind is fired by emotional power.[61] This level is the fourth of five stages during which an individual may develop his divine soul through contemplative awareness: from the initial acknowledgment of the spiritual truth of his contemplative theme to an "ecstasy of the whole essence ['atzmiyut]," in which "the being" of the worshipper "is so absorbed that nothing of himself remains and he has no self-consciousness whatever."[62] In special circumstances, such as martyrdom, the soul spark of this spiritual state radiates outward, an earthly hint of the soul's total withdrawal into God.[63]

On the basis of the Lurianic model noted earlier, one might therefore conclude that Dov Ber has two types of Shema recital in mind here: the first being the liturgical proclamation of the unity of God with the sincere intention to die a martyr and the other being its performance in the course of actual martyrdom. This relationship between theoretical and actual death in contemplative ecstasy would seem to accord with the fourth and fifth levels of ecstatic trance in the *Qunṭeres*. The fact that Dov Ber refers to the consummate mystical state as "the love of [God] 'with all your might'" also suggests that this ecstasy was somehow related to a recitation of the Shema. But the master does not say so. What Dov Ber actually does is transform the Lurianic hierarchy found in *Sha'ar ha-Kavvanot* and place the performance of the *nefilat 'appayim* rite on a higher level than the recital of the Shema. This reconception of the ladder of ecstatic ascension is revealed in his meditations on the *nefilat 'appayim* rite in *Sha'ar ha-Teshuvah veha-Tefillah*,[64] which has linguistic and thematic links with the *Qunṭeres*. Starting from the verse "(You shall follow the Lord, your God . . .) and serve Him and cleave to Him" (Deuteronomy 13:5), Dov Ber develops a hierarchy of states that may be achieved in the course of the liturgy.[65] The contemplative level attained through the *nefilat 'appayim* rite (indicated here by the words "and cleave to Him") is superior to that available through the Amidah prayer (indicated by "serve Him"), since the latter only achieves a temporary annihilation of the self and no permanent "cessation of one's entire essence [*'atzmuto*]." Unless the Amidah stage is the starting point for a deeper penetration into the divine Whole, the worshipper will gradually return to mundane reality and self-centeredness.[66] Only the *nefilat 'appayim* rite brings one to the state of supernormal consciousness that Dov Ber desires. Here the adept may be "absorbed [*nikhlal*] into the supernal Reality," becoming One with it (*ve-hayu le-'ahadim*), so that any trace of former separation is erased.[67] This deep *unio mystica* is deemed a permanent "bonding" (*hitqashsherut*) with God, an annihilation of the self into "the actual divine Reality" (*mahut 'eloqut mamash*).[68]

The superiority of the *nefilat 'appayim* state to that induced by the Shema recital reveals another dimension of this exalted level of mystical death in the thought of Dov Ber. Although this master recognized the spiritual heights possible through contemplating martyrdom while reciting the Shema and lauded those who were able to prepare for such a death in the liturgy and withstand its terrors in actuality,[69] the advantage of the *nefilat 'appayim* practice lies precisely in its conjunction of the theoretical and actual. Recalling the old zoharic rubric that one should consider oneself "as if" dead when performing *nefilat 'appayim,* Dov Ber says that "this is no mere act of imagination [*shi'ur*] but an 'actual seeming' [*dami mamash*]"; that is, when one truly gives oneself to death in the ritual, such that the merest "trace" of life is left, "this is no mere semblance [of death] produced by the imaginative faculty [*koah ha-medammeh*] but verity itself."[70] In such a state, that aspect of the worshipper's divine soul known as *yehidah* ascends on high, and he is virtually dead to this world, having entered a near-comatose state of "deep sleep" (*nirdam*). At this level of expiration, the ecstatic is insensate to himself and all pain − an intriguing link in the old chain that taught that persons truly cleaving to God do not feel the tortures of their martyrdom. But this is only one feature of the self-transformation induced by this state. The other is the movement outward from the divine depths to life itself, where the ecstatic is thoroughly attached to God in all his acts – come what will and come what may. In particular, the mystic is able to engage in workaday matters without falling from his high level.[71] In terms of tradition, Dov Ber stands in a long line of masters who practiced this modality of spiritual consciousness.[72] This capacity to be truly dead (to the world) while still alive (in it) seems to be the great merit of the *nefilat 'appayim* practice. Significantly, in his *Qunṭeres* Dov Ber also discusses the capacity of the individual whose soul-aspect of *yeḥidah* has been activated in the fifth level of ecstasy to work in the world *and* be (simultaneously) disengaged from it. This level of meditative trance is thus equivalent to the state available liturgically through the *nefilat 'appayim* practice. It is a complex consciousness that tries to conjoin the narrow ridge of contemplative inaction with the broad path of human interaction in this world. This tension between (mystical) solitariness and (social) solidarity was snapped by Rabbi Aaron of Staroselye, Dov Ber's contemporary and rival, who understood the *nefilat 'appayim* ritual to exact a higher price of disengagement from material pursuits, for fear that the bond with God be broken.[73] To "die" in the liturgy is thus an initiation into a divine acosmism – beyond time and space. For Dov Ber, on the other hand, such a death is rather the beginning of a messianic consciousness in the here and now.[74]

Jewish religiosity cultivated dimensions of death for the sake of higher levels of spiritual awareness. In some circles there was an interest in integrating these elements into consciousness in order to prepare for the spiritual trials of a martyr's death *and* to prepare for one's own natural death. The latter involved imaginative anticipations of this event so that one might die in perfect faith. As a by-product, these exercises also evoked self-reflection such that more normative spiritual goals were achieved. The glosses of Rabbi Shabbetai Sheftel Horowitz to the *Shenei Lukhot ha-Berit* provide a case in point. In the context of his father's reformulation of the (deathbed) confessional of his own father (Rabbi Abraham Halevi, in *'Emeq Berakhah*), the son adds:

Let a person choose some time while he is still in good health to isolate himself and confess the following long confession; and [when doing so] he should consider himself [*yaḥashov be-da'ato*] as if [*ke'ilu*] he were dying. . . . [Indeed] it is worthwhile for every spiritually aware person to make use of the following confession and follow this practice at least before every New Moon, which is [considered] a minor Day of Atonement, and fast the whole day as on the Ninth of Ab, with all its restrictions. He should [then] thoroughly examine his ways and cleave to the Shekhinah for at least one hour; and [during this meditation] he should have his eyes closed [and directed] earthward while his heart is directed upward [to God]. And he should think of his death and dying day and devote himself to die in love whenever God, be He praised, may will it. And [during this procedure] let him be robed in a prayer shawl and wear phylacteries and induce great enthusiasm in himself.[75]

Rabbi Shabbetai Sheftel then continues with the confessional itself and includes not only the readiness to die a martyr's death and the recitation of Psalm 25 but also the significant addition that if he die by torture or the fear of death overwhelms him and shakes his resolve, "let this confession which I hereby recite [while in sound mind and body] be *as if* I recited it at the hour of my death, word for word, with great concentration and much crying."

Ritual Simulation and Substitution

With this formulation, the deathbed confessional has been adapted to spiritual growth and development. To be sure, there is much pathos in the fear that the terrors of death may confuse the mind and destroy a lifetime of religious piety. And indeed, subsequent writers dealing with preparations for death and dying have formulated a legal "announcement" whereby the faithful publicly proclaim that any impious statement made at death's door is "null and void like a broken sherd" (*baṭṭel u-mevuṭṭal ke-ḥereś ha-nishbar*).[76] Similarly, Rabbi Naftali Katz in the early eighteenth century gives a poignant statement of popular fears concerning the devouring power of the Devil, who may appear to the moribund through "apparitions . . . and weird guises to confuse and frighten" the worshipper, and who may thereby induce in him a "madness" ending in apostasy.[77] All this accounts for the great concern for expressing the confession properly and in perfect faith *before* the onset of death's anxieties. But it does not fully account for the ritualization of death through periodic meditations in isolation, together with private penances and self-dedication. All this is part of a process of internalizing the prospect of death, so that life becomes an ongoing practicing of death. The transfer here of Psalm 25 (which Shabbetai Sheftel takes over from his forebears) gives added emphasis to the type of religious devotion involved.[78] Spiritual perfection involves a dedication of the earthly self to God, a recentering of the person in the divine Self. As an aid toward this, the worshipper is told to close his eyes in meditation. This involves more than an act of humility in prayer.[79] What is rather involved is a type of sensory deprivation induced so that the worshipper may "remove his thoughts from all matters of this world *as if* his soul had departed from him."[80] The practice of closing the eyes in meditation is thus a form of dying to the world so that the soul may cleave to God alone – a first level of withdrawal, seconded by the concentration upon death itself. In this way the "as if" becomes "real," and the ritual induces a spiritual metamorphosis in the celebrant.

One final document brings these austere considerations into focus. It teaches a spiritual practice of uncompromising intensity – one that attempts to bring life and death into the most fateful fusion for the sake of inner perfection. The text is the so-called *Tzetl Qotn* of the great nineteenth-century Tzaddik Rabbi Elimelekh of Lizensk.[81] Following common Hasidic custom, with roots in the medieval moral literature and earlier, Rabbi Elimelekh provides a list of spiritual practices (a kind of interior *regimen vitae*) that the adept is urged to study and internalize. The first two directives are of direct pertinence to our present discussion.

1. Whenever a person is not engaged in Torah study, and particularly when alone in his room or unable to sleep at night, let him think of the positive duty of "and I shall be sanctified among the people of Israel" [Leviticus 22:32]. And let him imagine in his soul and visualize in his mind *as if* [*ke'ilu*] a great and awesome fire burned before him up to the heart of heaven, and that he, for the sake of the sanctification of the Name, will overcome his nature and throw himself into the fire for the sanctification of the Name. And the Holy One, blessed be He, converts good thought into deeds [in his sight], so that the worshipper need not sit idly but may [even at such times] fulfill positive commands of the Torah.

2. A person should also think of the foregoing [meditation on death] during the first verse of the Shema and the first blessing of the Amidah. And he should also intend the following: [that] even if the gentile nations persecute him terribly and rake his flesh to force him to deny God's Unity – heaven

forbid! – he will endure these torments and never cower to them. And he will visualize in his mind *as if* [*ke'ilu*] they were doing the foregoing to him, and in that way [he will] properly fulfill the recitation of the Shema and Amidah prayers.

The work continues with the stark advice to have similar thoughts and intentions while eating, engaged in sexual intercourse, or during any other act of physical pleasure.

With this regimen, the imagination of death has absorbed the totality of one's life – filling the spaces of solitude; ensuring the validity of prayer; and even neutralizing essential acts of human satisfaction. For Rabbi Elimelekh, the ruins of the heart must be sanctified through sacrificial discipline. In this way the old martyrological ideal is transformed: God is not simply or only "sanctified among [*be-tokh*] the children of Israel" but *within* their very being. A purified inwardness thus supplements public resistance as the way to sanctify the Name. On this path, everything seen and tasted in the sensible world must be the occasion to "taste and see that the Lord is good" (Psalm 34:9), that His exalted Being is the Source of all appearance. This insight occurs in the heart; its cultivation through meditation and ritual is the very means to redemption. It is just here that visualizations of death play a pivotal role. Situated between external perception and inner vision, these formalized projections are designed to purify the heart and devote it solely to God. For Rabbi Elimelekh, the natural play of appearance is a mirror of base desire, trapping the self in its myriad reflections. The spiritual task is thus to free the soul from misprision – and to unify its focus. Gradually, through the screen of simulated death, the divine reality may come into view before the inner eye. And then the soul will be saved.

Epilogue

The lines of these various chapters trace the spiritual face of Judaism, in one of its many appearances. Behind the visage is a passion for religious perfection, expressed as the love of God unto death itself. The masters of the tradition cultivated this ideal in all periods, in diverse genres, and in different modes. Rabbinic law and midrash, medieval philosophy and mysticism, and public and private ritual all have their due in this development. Rooted in the understanding that the spiritual life requires discipline, the sages set up different ladders of ascension. For some, the Law itself (philosophically or mystically understood) was this means of spiritual growth; for others, more private practices were built upon its firm foundation. But all agreed that the purification of desire and the perfection of the soul offered the hope of personal salvation. None denied the historical redemption of the nation.

Two wings guided the flight of the soul: Moses' call to love God with all one's heart and soul and might (Deuteronomy 6:5) and the lover's desire for the kisses of her Beloved (Songs 1:2). The first is a positive religious duty, subject to obligation and routine, whereas the second breathes the pathos of unfulfilled longing. Together they center Jewish worship in its objective and subjective dimensions; in its capacity for ritual continuity and the revisions of radical interpretation. Empowered by love commanded and aroused, the meanings of love and their modes of expression underwent numerous permutations. These are the tropes of love which entwine the sources and open new spaces for the religious imagination. Indeed,

Epilogue

nothing so much impresses the onlooker as the way the Jewish exegetical imagination constructed models of action for the believer. Be these models the shape of spiritual growth or martyrological ideals, Judaism is characterized by the exegetical construction of reality. The layering of these constructions (in texts and practice) gives special depth to the unfolding tradition and provides a thicker version of historical theology than might otherwise be seen by the interpreter or comparativist.

A deep myth-ritual structure thus comes to view. On the one hand, the (biblical) interpretations of love construct theological ideals and ways to ritualize them. On the other, older rituals (routine or occasional, like the *nefilat 'appayim* rite or martyrdom) draw on existing theologies (or mythic theosophies) and concretize them. The living religious culture shuttles along this loom, spinning a tangle of meanings and behaviors that hold the worshipper in thrall. The spell is increased by the complexity of the elements. Where love and death are involved, paradoxical reciprocations abound on several registers – be these physical and spiritual (body and soul) or this world and another (historical and metaphysical reality). Thus, spiritual love may be confirmed or completed by social acts, even as spiritual expiry may be sealed or sanctified by social acts. A theology of atonement adds a more sacrificial dimension. Not only can physical death help atone for sins committed on earth, but a perfect martyrdom has the singular power to repair spiritual realities in the divine realm. At this level (as taught by ibn Gabbai and others), heavenly love is activated by human death. Self-sacrifice thus stands at the heart of Being – a sacrament of love for the salvation of God. A darker mystery is unimaginable.

Except for the human heart itself. The masters of the tradition acknowledge this in their many meditations on

Epilogue

the two *yetzers*, whose harmonization requires a deeper ritual of sacrifice in the worshipper. The two must become one through a transformation of base desire and its redirection to God alone in love. The ritualization of this process through halakhic discipline and meditative techniques allowed the quest to dominate the liturgical life of the Jew, shaping sensibilities with shared ideals. One need only recall that both the Shema recitation and the *nefilat 'appayim* rite were each practiced twice daily (along with other, affiliated practices) to appreciate the point; but the process extended to study and the wider purport of Judaism's ritual regime. Private practices supplemented this communal sphere in accordance with the specific character of the worshipper or the goals desired. In all cases, the chastening of passion was for the sake of personal perfection. Only in this state could the soul be released from its earthly prison – whether to ascend to its Source in heaven or become a shrine for the holy Spirit. Death to the vagaries of the self is thus a nullification of the division separating the soul from God – recentering the soul in the divine Self. For the seeker, this is a divine kiss.

Notes

Introduction

1. See M. Weinfeld, *Deuteronomy and the Deuteronomic School* (Oxford: Clarendon Press, 1972), 81–85, following W. L. Moran, "The Ancient Near Eastern Background of Love of God in Deuteronomy," *Catholic Biblical Quarterly* 25 (1963): 77–78.

2. This is how the Septuagint and Vulgate interpreted it. The New Testament follows this tradition, along with the significant addition "with all your mind" (*en bolē tē dianoia su,* Luke 10:27; cf. Mark 12:30). This is undoubtedly a lost midrashic reading of *me'odekha* (your might) as *mada'akha* (your mind); cf. the Hebrew translation of F. Delitzsch. For other midrashic plays, see the continuation of the *Sifrei Deuteronomy* 32 passage (ed. L. Finkelstein [New York: Jewish Theological Seminary of America, 1969], 55) and *M. Berakhot* IX. 5.

3. Material wealth is the meaning given in *M. Berakhot* IX. 5, Targum Onqelos, Targum Jonathan, and the Peshiṭta.

4. A comprehensive review of rabbinic remarks on the two inclinations can be found in E. E. Urbach, *The Sages* (Cambridge, Mass.: Harvard University Press, 1987), 471–83.

5. See esp. the *Testaments of the Twelve Patriarchs,* in *The Old Testament Pseudepigrapha,* ed. J. Charlesworth (Garden City, N.Y: Doubleday, 1983), 1:816–18 (The Testament of Asher). For the Greek text, see *Testamenta XII Patriarcharum,* ed. M. de Jonge (Leiden: E. J. Brill, 1964), 63–65.

6. E.g., Ben Sira 33:7–18; *M. Abot* II.1, 9; *Mekhilta de-Rabbi Ishmael* on Exodus 14:29 (ed. H. Horowitz and I. Rabin [Jerusalem: Bamberger and Wahrmann, 1960], 112); and various minor tractates on ethics. See also D. Flusser, "'Eizo Hiy Derekh Yesharah She-Yavor Bo 'Adam (*Abot* II.1)," *Tarbiz* 60 (1991): 163–78.

7. See 1QS II.13–IV.14; and J. Licht, "An Analysis of the Treatise on the Two Spirits in DSD," *Scripta Hierosolymitana* 4 (1958): 87–100. Flusser ("'Eizo Hiy Derekh Yesharah," 167)

has compared the "theoretical speculations" in 1QS III.20–21 and IV.2, 18 with the Didache.

8. But see *Genesis Rabba* 14.4 (ed. J. Theodor and C. Albeck [Jerusalem: Wahrmann Books, 1965], 128), where the two yods of *vayiytzer*, "[the Lord God] created," in Genesis 2:7 are interpreted to indicate that the two *yetzers* are primordial creations of God.

9. In the Finkelstein edition, p. 55. Cf. *Sifrei Deuteronomy* 31 (Finkelstein edition, p. 53), where the noun *maḥloqet* is used by the patriarch Jacob on his deathbed when he asks his sons if they have any "conflict" in their hearts toward God. They respond by reciting Deuteronomy 6:4 (punning on Jacob as Israel); Jacob's reference to "your hearts" alludes to Deuteronomy 6:5. The sons aver their wholehearted devotion to the one God.

10. The use of *bekhol* (all) in a distributive sense (every) is common.

11. The idea of "wholehearted" service is stated in *Midrash Deuteronomy Rabba*, ed. S. Lieberman (Jerusalem: Wahrmann Books, 1974), 70, where also the reading of the explication is "that your heart not be divided *with you* [*'aleykha*]." For other instances of this reading, see S. Lieberman, *Kirjath Sefer* 14 (1938): 332.

12. *Tosefta* VI.7 (line 37), in *Tosefta: Zera'im*, ed. S. Liebermann (New York: Jewish Theological Seminary of America, 1955), 35.

13. See *Mekhilta de-Rabbi Ishmael, de-Shira* 3 (Horowitz-Rabin edition, p. 127).

14. Cf. Rashi, ad loc. "The evil inclination is as much as dead within me, for it is in my power to suppress it."

15. The combat motif is quite common. Cf. two sayings of R. Resh Lakish: "One should always incite the good inclination against the evil one [Rashi glosses: He should wage war against the evil inclination]. . . . If he conquers him, fine; if not, let him study Torah" (*b. Berakhot* 5a); and "A person's [evil] *yetzer* gathers strength each day and seeks to slay him . . . ; and were it not that the Holy One, blessed be He, comes to his aid, he would not overcome it" (*b. Qiddushin* 30b).

16. Jerome learned this interpretation from a Jewish teacher, who taught it in the name of R. Akiba. See L. Ginzberg, "Die Haggada bei den Kirchvätern," in *Abhandlungen zur*

Erinnerung an H. P. Chayes (Vienna: A. Kohut Memorial Foundation, 1933), 30.

17. Underlying the image is the rabbinic teaching that the 248 parts of the human body correspond to the 248 positive commandments of the Torah (*b. Makkot* 23*b*; cf. *M. Oholot* I.8). Together with the 365 negative commandments, corresponding to the days of the solar year, there developed a tally of 613 commandments given to Moses. The sages gave strong homiletic expression to this idea (see *Pesiqta de-Rav Kahana* 12.1 [ed. B. Mandelbaum (New York: Jewish Theological Seminary of America, 1962), 1:203]) and even "found" it alluded to in the 613 words of the Decalogue (*Midrash Bereshit Rabbati,* ed. C. Albeck [Jerusalem: Mekize Nirdamim, 1940], 8). This tradition may derive from R. Saadia Gaon; see Urbach, *The Sages,* 362.

18. For the Hebrew text and other translations, see *Selected Poems of Jehudah Halevi,* ed. H. Brody, trans. N. Salaman (Philadelphia: Jewish Publication Society, 1924), 84–86; and *The Penguin Book of Hebrew Verse,* ed. and trans. T. Carmi (New York: Penguin Books, 1981), 336–37.

19. For this contrast, see also R. Solomon ibn Gabirol, in *Shirei Qodesh le-Rabbi Shlomo ben Yehuda ibn Gabirol,* ed. H. N. Bialik and Y. H. Ravnitzky (Tel Aviv: Devir, 1925), 3:253 ('*ayin; siman* 112); and R. Moses ibn Ezra, *Shirei ha-Qodesh,* ed. S. Bernstein (Tel Aviv: Masada, 1957), 48 (third stanza). For the juxtaposition of *yetzer* and *tzar* (enemy) to the *'otzar* (treasury) of God, see R. Yehuda Alḥarizi, *Sefer ha-'Anaq,* ed. A. Avronin (Tel Aviv: Maḥberot Lesifrut, 1945), *siman* II.

20. In a stark pun, R. Moses ibn Ezra calls upon God to "behold the prisoner ['*asir*]" whose heart smolders "like a pot [*sir*]" (*Shirei ha-Qodesh,* 145). Elsewhere, Yehuda Halevi speaks of the soul as a prisoner (*'asir*) and the world as a dungeon (*kele'*); see *Shirei ha-Qodesh le-Rabbi Yehuda Halevi,* ed. D. Yarden (Jerusalem, 1982), 3:723.

21. The topos recalls R. Yitzḥaq ibn Ghiyyat's line, "O Lord! my soul dies [*tikhleh*] to escape from my house of sorrow ['*anḥati*] to my [heavenly] house of rest [*hanaḥati*] / O Lord! all my desire is toward You" (*Siftei Renanot* [Gerba, 1947], 2:12).

22. In the words of R. Yannai: "Whoever listens to his [evil] *yetzer* is, as it were, an idolater. For what reason? [Scripture, which says:] 'There shall be no strange god in thee; neither shall

thou worship any foreign god' [Psalm. 81:10]. [That means:] Do not make the stranger within you your sovereign" (*j. Nedarim* IX.1.41*a*). For a poignant, stylized "debate" between the two *yetzers*, see the thirteenth- to fourteenth-century poem "Vikuaḥ beyn Yetzer Ṭov ve-Yetzer Ra'," ed. A. M. Haberman, *Tarbiz* 50 (1980–81): 450–55.

1. "If you wish to live, then die"
Aspects of Death and Desire in Jewish Spirituality

1. See *Song of Songs Rabba* to Songs 1:1 (1.2.xi); *Leqaḥ Tov,* ed. A. W. Greenup (London, 1909), 9; and the Targum ad loc.

2. *Songs Rabba* 1.2.viii.

3. Cf. ibid., 1.9.vi.

4. Ibid., 1.2.ii, for the complex of traditions involved. The issues have been variously discussed in connection with Origen and Christian traditions. See E. E. Urbach, "The Homiletical Interpretation of the Sages and the Expositions of Origen on Canticles, and the Jewish Christian Disputation," *Scripta Hierosolymitana* 22 (1971): 254–56; R. Kimelman, "Rabbi Yohanan and Origen on the Song of Songs," *Harvard Theological Review* 73 (1980): 574–77 and n. 47; and recently, M. Hirschman, *Ha-Miqra' u-Midrasho* (Tel Aviv: Hakibbutz Hameuchad, 1991), 70–72.

5. E.g., *Exodus Rabba* 29.4, 9; *Numbers Rabba* 10.1.

6. *b. Shabbat* 88*b*. And see also *Mekhilta de-Rabbi Ishmael, Ba-Ḥodesh* 9 (Horowitz-Rabin edition, p. 236), where a tradition is reported in the name of R. Judah b. Ilai that God commanded the clouds of Glory to sprinkle Israel with *ṭal ḥayyim*, "the dew of life," in order to revive them from the scorching heat of the revelation. By saying that the Israelites were *meshulahavin*, "scorched," by the heavenly *'esh*, "fire," the midrash strongly alludes to Songs 8:6, which says that the *'esh* of love is a scorching (or divine-like) fire (*shalhevetyah*).

7. I. Chernus, *Mysticism in Rabbinic Judaism* (Berlin and New York: W. de Gruyter, 1982), chaps. 3–4, has suggested that these traditions indicate "initiatory death." I am unconvinced. On the other hand, his demonstration of the softening of the

divine Word in the developing tradition to accommodate human capacity is compelling.

8. *Pesiqta Rabbati* 20.4 (ed. M. Ish Shalom [Vienna, 1880], 98*b*).

9. See my overall discussion in "The 'Form' of God's Appearance in the Ancient Midrash," in *Messiah and Christos: Festschrift for David Flusser,* ed. I. Gruenwald, S. Shaked, and G. Stroumsa (Tübingen: J. C. B. Mohr, 1992), 53–74.

10. See A. Jellinek, *Bet ha-Midrash* (reprint, Jerusalem: Wahrmann Books, 1967), 1:113–29. For sources and studies on the Death of Aaron, see H. Schwarzbaum, "Jewish, Christian, Moslem and Falasha Legends of the Death of Aaron," in his *Jewish Folklore between East and West* (Beer Sheva, Israel: Ben Gurion University Press, 1989), 31–73.

11. See the *piyyuṭim* in L. Weinberger, "The Death of Moses in the Synagogue Liturgy" (Ph.D. diss., Brandeis University, 1963), nos. 6, 27, 49, 53, 61, 68, 72, 75.

12. To achieve this, the rabbis boldly replace biblical *gevim,* "grasshoppers," with rabbinic *gabbin,* "cisterns."

13. Cf. Porphyry, *Sententiae ad intelligibilia ducentes,* ed. B. Mommert (Leipzig: B. G. Tuebner, 1907), ix: "Death is twofold, one known by all when body is loosed from soul, the other that of the philosophers where the soul is loosed from the body."

14. See Philo of Alexandria, *De Specialibus Legibus* (The Special Laws) I.48.257. On the idea of "practicing death," cf. the idiom *meletōsai . . . apothnēskein,* "Study to die (to the life of the body)," in Philo of Alexandria, *De Gigantibus* (On the Giants) III.14; and Plato, *Phaedo* 67E, *apothnēskein meletōsi.* See *Philo II,* ed. F. Colson (Loeb Classical Library, 1927; reprint, 1979), appendix, p. 502.

15. Philo of Alexandria, *Legum Allegoria* (Allegorical Interpretation) II.57–58, and *De Somnis* (On Dreams) II.67. The sons die a mystical-spiritual death in rabbinic literature also; see *Leviticus Rabba* 12.2 and the comment of R. Ḥayyim ibn 'Aṭṭar cited below (n. 69).

16. Philo of Alexandria, *De Fuga et Inventione* (On Flight and Finding) 59.

17. See *The Book of the Gests of Alexander of Macedon,* ed. and trans. I. Kazis (Cambridge, Mass.: Medieval Academy of America, 1962).

18. Ḥunayn ibn Isḥaq, *Sefer Muserei ha-Pilosofim,* ed. A. Loewenthal (Berlin: J. Kauffman, 1896), 88.

19. See N. Brüll, "Verschollene Boraita's und Midraschim," *Jahrbücher für jüdischer Geschichte und Literatur* 2 (1876): 129.

20. *Vida y Obras de San Juan del la Cruz,* ed. C. de Jesus (Madrid: Biblioteca de Autores Cristianos, 1946), 1245–46. See also A. M. Haas, *Sermo Mysticus: Studien zu Theologie und Sprache der deutschen Mystik* (Freiburg: Universitätsverlag, 1979), 425, as well as the many other Christian examples of *"mors mystica"* considered (pp. 392–480). On this topos (including the words of St. John of the Cross), see also R. J. Zwi Werblowsky, *Joseph Karo: Lawyer and Mystic* (Philadelphia: Jewish Publication Society, 1977), 252 and notes.

21. *Isaac Israeli: A Neoplatonic Philosopher of the Early Tenth Century,* trans. with comments by A. Altmann and A. M. Stern (Oxford: Oxford University Press, 1958), 26.

22. See Shem Ṭov's commentary to the *Guide,* ad loc. III. 51 (68a, Warsaw ed.). For the expression and extensive discussion, see R. Lerner, "Maimonides' Governance of the Solitary," in *Perspectives on Maimonides: Philosophical and Historical Studies,* ed. J. Kraemer (Oxford: Oxford University Press, 1991), 33–46.

23. S. Pines, trans., *The Guide of the Perplexed* (Chicago: University of Chicago Press, 1963). I have followed the translation of Pines throughout. On the broad theme of the kiss of God in contemporary Christian sources, see N. Perella, *The Kiss, Sacred and Profane: An Interpretative History of Kiss Symbolism and Related Religio-erotic Themes* (Berkeley and Los Angeles: University of California Press, 1969), passim. The kiss of God is a central feature in the works of the great contemporary Christian mystic Bernard of Clairvaux. See his *Sermones Super Cantica Canticorum,* esp. I. vi. 12, III. iii. 5, IV. i. 1, VIII. 1. 1–VIII. 8. On other aspects, see I. Löw, "Der Kuss," *Monatsschrift für die Geschichte und Wissenschaft des Judentums* 65 (1921): 253ff.; and G. Stälin, *Theologische Wörterbuch zum Alten Testament* (Stuttgart: Kohlhammer, 1975), 9:125–26, s.v. *Phileō.*

24. *Falaquera's Book of the Seeker (Sefer ha-Mebaqqesh),* ed. M. Herschel Levine (New York: Yeshiva University Press, 1976), 61–62.

25. See *Shelemut ha-Ma'asim,* chap. 9; in the edition of R. Jospe, *Torah and Sophia: The Life and Thought of Shem Tov ibn Falaquera*

(Cincinnati: Hebrew Union College Press, 1988), 435, line 15.

26. The point is made by Jospe, *Torah and Sophia*, 141.

27. *Iggeret ha-Ḥalom* (see H. Malter, "Shem Tov ben Joseph Palquera: His 'Treatise of the Dream,'" *Jewish Quarterly Review*, n.s. 1 [1910/11]: 484). For further on the subject of asceticism in Judaism, see the discussion and new texts published by D. Schwartz, "Asceticism and Self-mortification: Attitudes Held by a Provençal Circle of Commentators of the *Kuzari*," *Meḥqarei Yerushalayim be-Maḥshevet Yiśrael* 11 (1993): 79–99 (Hebrew).

28. Moses ibn Tibbon, *Peirush 'al Shir ha-Shirim*, ed. Lyck, (Jerusalem: Mekize Nirdamim, 1874), 14.

29. *Peirush le-Rabbi Yitzḥaq ibn Sahula*, ed. A. Green, in *Meḥqarei Yerushalayim be-Maḥshevet Yiśrael* 6, nos. 3–4 (1988): 410.

30. Isaac ibn Laṭif, *Tzeror ha-Mor*, chap. 6; see in A. Jellinek, *Kerem Ḥemed* 9 (1856): 157.

31. *The Epistle on the Possibility of the Conjunction with the Active Intellect by ibn Rushd with the Commentary of Moses Narboni*, ed. and trans. K. Bland (New York: Jewish Theological Seminary of America, 1982), 96. See also the comment of Prat Maimon to *Batei ha-Nefesh*, "but one who departs (this life) with a kiss is happy, for his death is (true) life for him," in Schwartz, "Asceticism and Self-mortification," 83 (ad folio 53a).

32. *Kitvei Rabbenu Baḥye*, ed. H. Chavel (Jerusalem: Mosad Ha-Rav Kook, 1971), 35.

33. Both passages are cited in *Guide* III.51 (Pines, p. 622).

34. Ibid., III.51 (p. 621).

35 The pertinent section of the manuscript *Sodot* (Bibliothèque national, Paris, MS. 790, fols. 141a–b) has been printed and translated by M. Idel in "Music and Prophetic Kabbalah," *Yuval* 4 (1982): 161–62; and also in his *The Mystical Experience in Abraham Abulafia* (Albany: SUNY Press, 1988), 60–61 (see also his chap. 2).

36. *Sefer Me'irat 'Einayim le-Rabbi Yitzḥaq de-min 'Acco*, critical edition by A. Goldreich (Jerusalem, 1981), 217 (102b).

37. Ibid., 213 (100b).

38. Ibid., 217 (103a–b; end and beginning).

39. *Guide* III.51 (Pines, pp. 624–28); but he speaks of "one

endowed with perfect apprehension, whose intellect never ceases from being occupied with God."

40. The verb *bala‘* is obviously difficult. Since antiquity the sense of covering has been attributed to it (see Targum Onqelos, Saadia, Rashi, Rashbam, and ibn Ezra), particularly as an act accomplished while dismantling the Tabernacle for transport (see Rashbam, ibn Ezra, and Ḥizkuni). The destructive aspect of the verb (following Lamentations 2:2) has been correctly noted by Rashbam and especially Ḥizkuni.

41. *'Otzar Ḥayyim*, MS. Moscow-Günzberg 775, fol. 111*a*; cited and discussed in E. Gottlieb, *Meḥqarim be-Sifrut ha-Kabbalah*, ed. J. Hacker (Tel Aviv: Tel Aviv University Press, 1977), 237; and by M. Idel, *Kabbalah: New Perspectives* (New Haven: Yale University Press, 1988), 70–71, as an example of "the swallowing metaphor."

42. Gottlieb (*Meḥqarim be-Sifrut ha-Kabbalah*) considers the passage an example of *hit'aḥdut mamash*, "actual unitive (experience)"; so does Idel (*Kabbalah*), without however noting the death aspect per se. This point is crucial to the proof text and thus, I believe, to Rabbi Isaac's understanding.

43. *'Otzar Ḥayyim*, fol. 161*b*. The motif is adduced by Idel (*Kabbalah*, 67) in connection with oceanic metaphors.

44. MS. Vatican 283, fol. 71*b*, published by I. Tishby, *Commentary on Talmudic Aggadoth by Rabbi Azriel of Gerona*, 2d ed. (Jerusalem: Magnes Press, 1982), Introduction, 19 (Hebrew pagination).

45. See E. E. Urbach, "Ha-Mesorot 'al Torat ha-Sod be-Tequfat ha-Tannaim," in *Studies in Mysticism and Religion Presented to Gershom G. Scholem* (Jerusalem: Magnes Press, 1968), 1–27.

46. *j. Ḥagiga* 77*b*; *Songs Rabba* 1:4.

47. See also *Tos. Ḥagiga* II.3–4.

48. I am persuaded by the form-critical conclusion of D. Halperin, *The Merkabah in Rabbinic Literature* (New Haven: American Oriental Society, 1980), 91–92. Despite his cautions, I tend to regard the locus of the *pardes* in some heavenly realm.

49. See also *Tos. Ḥagiga* II.3–4, except for MS. Erfurt.

50. Pride is the sin of Elisha according to Y. Liebes, *Ḥeṭ'o shel Elisha* (Jerusalem: Akademon Press, 1990), esp. chap. 3.

51. Liebes (ibid., 94–95) also notes the positive evaluation

of the mystic's death and suggests that the verse was added to the Talmud on the basis of ben Azzai's own interpretation in *Genesis Rabba* 62.2 that the righteous receive a divine reward "near their death." I do not think that this is the force of the proof text in the Talmud.

52. Menaḥem Recanati, *Peirush 'al ha-Torah* (Venice, 1545), fol. 77c–d.

53. Ibid., fol. 77c.

54. So G. Scholem, *Ursprung und Anfänge der Kabbala* (Berlin: Walter de Gruyter, 1962), 268–69. The reference is to Rabbi Azriel's *Commentary on Talmudic Aggadoth*, 40 (see n. 44).

55. Discussed by Idel, *Kabbala*, 75–88.

56. See R. Schatz-Uffenheimer, *Ha-Ḥasidut ke-Mystiqa* (Jerusalem: Magnes Press, 1968), 42–43.

57. The printed edition reads *parṣa'*; Recanati reads *'arṣa'*.

58. Recanati glosses here: "So you can see that because of the intensity of the conjunction of their souls to the Upper Soul they died the death of the kiss" (*Peirush 'al ha-Torah*, fol. 78c).

59. *be-shalom;* lit., "(physically and spiritually) whole" or "intact." Through the formulations of Recanati, the theme of death by kiss entered the Christian Kabbala of the Renaissance – notably the *morte di bacio* (*mors osculi*) of Pico della Mirandola. See Chaim Wirszubski, *Sheloshah Peraqim be-Toledot ha-Qabbala ha-Notzrit* (Tel Aviv: Mosad Bialik, 1975), 16–22. He also notes the influence of Plato's *Symposium,* pars. 211–12.

60. For a similar evaluation and a translation of ibn Sahula's comment, see the discussion in A. Green, "The Song of Songs in Jewish Mysticism," *Orim* 2, no. 2 (1987): 57–58.

61. MS. Oxford 1582, fol. 52a.

62. Ibid., fol. 14b. "And truly whoever's soul departs from him when pronouncing [the divine Name], he will die by a kiss; and thus they have said [about] Rabbi Akiba, that his soul departed [when he said,] 'One.'" On the motif of Akiba's passion, see below, chapter 2.

63. *Sefer ha-Malmad,* MS. Oxford 1649, fol. 207a, cited and translated in Idel, *The Mystical Experience in Abraham Abulafia,* 177, n. 347.

64. *Gan Na'ul,* MS. Munich 58, fols. 317a–b. The full passage is cited and translated in Idel, *The Mystical Experience in Abraham Abulafia,* 142–43. I am grateful to my friend Moshe

Idel for making a copy of this and other manuscripts of Abulafia available to me.

65. Idel (*The Mystical Experience of Abraham Abulafia*, 143) translates *mitqayyemin* (realized) as "preserved." The Maimonidean reference is to *Sefer ha-Mada': Hilkhot Talmud Torah* III.12 (not *Yesodei ha-Torah*).

66. Chapters 7–9 were published by G. Scholem, "Peraqim mi-*Sefer Sullam ha-'Aliyah* le-Rabbi Yehuda Albuṭini," *Kirjath Sefer* 22 (1945–46): 161–71. Scholem indicates the strong influence of Abulafia's *Sefer 'Or ha-Sekhel* and *Sefer Ḥayyei ha-'Olam ha-Ba'*. Chapter 10 was published in *Kitvei Yad be-Qabbalah*, addendum to *Kirjath Sefer* 7 (1930–31): 225–30. The influence of *Ḥayyei ha-'Olam ha-Ba'* begins on p. 226 (bottom); see n. 5 there. The entire text of *Sullam ha-'Aliyah* has recently been issued by Makhon Sha'arei Ziv (Jerusalem, 1989). Albuṭini was also influenced by the anonymous thirteenth-century tract *Sha'arei Tzedeq*; see Scholem, "'Sha'arei Tzedeq,' Ma'amar be-Qabbalah, me-'Askolat R. Avraham Abulafia, Meyuḥas le-R. Shem Ṭov (ibn Gaon?)," *Kirjath Sefer* 1 (1925): 138.

67. The term *hitboddedut* often means ascetical withdrawal or isolation, but in contexts like ours it means mental concentration. See P. Fenton, "La 'Hitbodedut' chez les premiers Qabbalists en Orient et chez les Soufis," in *Prière, mystique et Judaïsme,* ed. R. Goetschel (Paris: Presses Universitaires de France, 1987), 133–57; M. Idel, "Ha-Hitboddedut ke-Rikkuz ba-Qabbalah ha-Eqstatit ve-Gilguleyha," *Da'at* 14 (1986): 35–71; and cf. idem, "*Hitboddedut* as Concentration in Ecstatic Kabbala," in *Jewish Spirituality,* ed. A. Green (New York: Crossroad, 1986), vol. 1, chap. 15. Fenton's study demonstrates the remarkable similarities between Jewish and Sufic traditions and the possibility of Sufic influences.

68. *j. Shekalim* 3.4.47c; cf. M. Soṭa IX.15, with a slightly different ending. The Babylonian tradition in *b. Avoda Zara* 20b is without the eschatological conclusion and may be more authentic than the Mishnah. See Y. N. Epstein, *Mavo' le-Nusaḥ ha-Mishnah* (Jerusalem, 1948), 976–77.

69. For a quite remarkable and striking reversal of this method of dealing with the experience, note the discussion of R. Ḥayyim ibn 'Aṭṭar (1696–1743) in his Pentateuch commentary *'Or ha-Ḥayyim* where he refers to the death of the sons

of Aaron, who "approached [*be-qorvatam lifnei*] the Lord." A positive, mystical reading of this passage dates back to Philo and occurs in the Midrash (see above, n. 15); but the *'Or ha-Hayyim* goes further. Focusing on the verb of approach, he says that the sons were spiritually enthused with the supernal light and died in the mystery of the kiss. Their deaths differed from those of other righteous saints insofar as the latter waited for the divine kiss to come to them, whereas the sons of Aaron actually approached it. Indeed, ibn 'Attar concludes, even the orthography of the biblical verse hints that these lovers of God did not "break off their approach" to an ultimate cleaving to God "even though they [fully] sensed their [imminent] death." They thus chose to die while in ecstasy and did not withdraw to a this-worldly existence.

70. The crucial part IV, long deleted by printers, has been recently printed in *Ketavim Hadashim le-Rabbi Hayyim Vital* (Jerusalem: Ahavat Shalom Institute, 1989).

71. On the role of the imagination in *Sha'arei Qedushah* III. 5, see Werblowsky, *Joseph Karo*, 69–71.

72. *Maggid Mesharim*, 3d ed. (Amsterdam, 1698), 25b; cf. Werblowsky, *Joseph Karo*, 252, and the discussion of the whole passage (pp. 252–53).

73. See chapter 3.

74. *Tzeva'at ha-Ribash*, no. 43a.

75. *Zikhron Zo't, Beha'alotekha* (Brooklyn, N.Y., 1981), 29c. My translation differs slightly from that found in Idel, *Kabbala*, 69, where the focus is on the relationship between cleaving and death.

76. Idel (*Kabbala*, 69–70) sees the invocation of Leviticus 18:5 as a negation of mystical anomism.

77. *Maggid Devarav le-Ya'akov*, ed. R. Schatz-Uffenheimer (Jerusalem: Magnes Press, 1977), sermon 205.

78. *Hayyim Nahman Bialik: Shirim (1899–1934)*, critical edition by D. Miron et al. (Tel Aviv: Dvir, 1990), 2:205–9. (The poem was published in 1905; the critical edition follows the 1933 version.)

2. "For Your sake we are killed all day long"
The Sanctification of God in Love

1. Moshe Galante, *Kohelet Ya'aqov* (Safed, 1578), 73a. I have translated the biblical passage to reflect the intent of the exegesis. In context, the *mitzvah* refers to the command of a human king (see vv. 2–3).

2. Shimshon ben Zadok, *Tashbetz* (Cremona, 1557), par. 415; in the *Responsa of Rabbi Meir of Rothenberg* (ShuT MaHaRaM, Prague), par. 517.

3. This is also the opinion of R. Peretz of Corbeille (who considered himself a student of Rabbi Meir) in his glosses to the *Tashbetz*. See D. Tamar, "Peraqim le-Toledot Ḥakhmei 'Eretz Yiśrael ve-'Italiya ule-Toledot Sifrutam," *Kirjath Sefer* 33 (1958): 376, and idem, "'Od le-Ma'amaro shel MaHaRaM mi-Rotenberg be-'Inyan Qiddush ha-Shem," *Kirjath Sefer* 34 (1959): 376–77; reprinted in idem, *Meḥqarim be-Toledot ha-Yehudim be-'Eretz Yiśrael ube-'Italiya* (Jerusalem: R. Mas, 1986), 107, 112.

4. MS. Oxford 2295, fols. 1–2; published by G. Scholem in "Peraqim be-Toledot Sifrut ha-Qabbalah," *Kirjath Sefer* 7 (1930–31): 152–55. Scholem published a German translation earlier under the title "Rabbi Abraham ben Elieser Halewi: Über den Tod der Märtyrer," in *Festgabe für Martin Buber: Aus unbekannten Schriften* (Berlin, 1928), 89–94.

5. See pp. 32–33.

6. Scholem ("Peraqim be-Toledot Sifrut ha-Qabbalah," 441) already surmised that the "tradition of the sages" mentioned by Rabbi Abraham is the testimony of Rabbi Meir of Rothenberg.

7. See Y. Baer, "Gezerot TaTeNU," in *Sefer Asaf* (Jerusalem, 1954), 139, nn. 5–7.

8. I have translated in accord with the implied sense and pun on *mitpareqet* (shattered); see below.

9. Lit., "apple orchard" – a common Kabbalistic metaphor for paradise.

10. See Scholem, "Peraqim be-Toledot Sifrut ha-Qabbalah," 150, though he suggests that only 8:5–6 were used. The *Midrash ha-Ne'elam* clearly refers to Songs 6:9, where "mother" occurs. The reference in the Margoliot edition wrongly indicates 3:6 for 8:5.

11. Citations will follow the edition of A. Green; see chapter 1, n. 29.

12. Rabbi Abraham says *ki nifla't 'ahavatekha;* ibn Sahula remarks, *ki nifla'ah 'ahavatah.*

13. See the remarks of I. Gruenwald, "Qiddush ha-Shem: Beiruro shel Musag," *Molad* 24 (1967–68): 476–84; and S. Safrai, "Qiddush ha-Shem be-Toratam shel ha-Tannaim," *Zion* 44 (1979): 28–32. As an example of the sanctification of the divine Name (*Qiddush ha-Shem*) denoting divine honor, cf. in the *Mekhilta de-Rabbi Ishmael, Vayehi Be-Shallaḥ* 5 (Horowitz-Rabin edition, p. 107), where the midrash discusses the act of sanctification of Naḥshon ben Amminadav (of the tribe of Judah) together with a remarkable rereading of Psalm 114:2; see also *Sifrei Zuṭṭa* 7.11, in *Siphre d'Be Rab,* ed. H. S. Horowitz (Jerusalem: Wahrmann Books, 1966), 252.

14. See Safrai, "Qiddush ha-Shem be-Toratam shel ha-Tannaim," 32–42.

15. *de-Shira* 3 (Horowitz-Rabin edition, p. 127).

16. To achieve the meaning *'ad mavet* (to death) from *'alamot* (maidens), the latter is construed as from *'al mut* (or *'al mavet*). This teaching transforms Psalm 48:15, "For God – who is our God forever [*'olam va'ed*] – will lead us *'al mut* [beyond death]." This somewhat postbiblical theology (achieved via the vocalization) may itself transform an original *'olamot* (evermore). The Septuagint has this sense (*eistous aionas*), whereas the Syriac renders the Massoretic text quite literally (*l'l mn mwt'*); cf. Jerome's *in mortem.*

17. The words *metim* and *neheragin* (see quotation) set up the citations from Songs 1:3 and Psalm 44:23.

18. See S. Lieberman, "Mishnat Shir ha-Shirim," appendix D, in G. Scholem, *Jewish Gnosticism, Merkabah Mysticism and Talmudic Tradition* (New York: Jewish Theological Seminary of America, 1960), esp. p. 123.

19. *Sifra, 'Aharei Mot* XIII.14 (ed. I. Weiss [Vienna, 1862]); and cf. the reading in *Sifra or Torat Kohanim according to Codex Assemani LXVI,* ed. L. Finkelstein (New York: Jewish Theological Seminary of America, 1956), 374.

20. *Pesiqta de-Rav Kahana, pisqa* VII (ed. B. Mandelbaum [New York: Jewish Theological Seminary of America, 1962], 1:189).

21. *Midrash Tehillim*, ed. S. Buber (Vilna, 1891), 71*a* (on Psalm 18). *Tammati* hints at "death in purity."

22. Ibid., 46*a* (on Psalm 9).

23. *Songs Rabba*, VII.1.ix.

24. Following M. Schatkin, "The Maccabeean Martyrs," *Vigilae Christianae* 28 (1974): 98.

25. Y. Guttmann, "Ha-'Em ve-Shiv'at Baneyha ba-'Aggadah ube-Sifrei Hashmona'im II Ve-IV," in *Sefer Yoḥanan Levi*, ed. M. Schwabe and J. Guttman (Jerusalem: Magnes Press, 1949), 34–35.

26. Ibid., 25–27. For different versions, note the Franco-German recension of *Lamentations Rabba* (on 1:16); the Babylonian version in *b. Giṭṭin* 57*b*; and the different account in *Pesiqta Rabbati* XLIII (ed. M. Ish Shalom [Vienna, 1880], 180*b*).

27. The influence of the martyrological literature is cogently argued by G. Cohen, "Hannah and Her Seven Sons in Hebrew Literature," in *Studies in the Variety of Jewish Cultures* (Philadelphia: Jewish Publication Society, 1991), 39–60; the essay originally appeared in Hebrew in 1953.

28. S. Lieberman, "Redifot Dat Yiśrael," in *Salo Baron Jubilee Volume* (Jerusalem: American Academy of Jewish Research, 1976), pt. III, 234–45 (Hebrew section).

29. I am indebted to Lieberman (ibid., 222–28) for raising the issue of the more legendary character of this pericope as compared with that in the Jerusalem Talmud (cited below).

30. Following Lieberman, ibid., 225.

31. Ibid., 227.

32. *b. Avoda Zara* 27*b*.

33. *b. Sanhedrin* 68*a*.

34. The different versions have now been gathered and critically edited by G. Reeg, *Die Geschichte von den zehn Märtyrern* (Tübingen: J. C. B. Mohr, 1985).

35. Vatican MS. Ebr. 285 is recension VII in Reeg; the manuscript was first published by M. Hirschler, "Midrash 'Aśarah Harugei Malkhut," *Sinai* 71 (1974): 218–28.

36. I cite from *Sefer Gezerot Ashkenaz ve-Tzarefat*, ed. A. M. Haberman (Jerusalem: Ophir, 1972), 31.

37. I. Marcus, in his review of R. Chazan, *European Jewry and the First Crusade* (Berkeley and Los Angeles: University of California Press, 1987), 686. A fuller development of his

argument, entitled "History, Story and Collective Memory: Narrativity and Early Ashkenazi Culture," can be found in *The Midrashic Imagination,* ed. M. Fishbane (Albany: SUNY Press, 1993), along with essays by R. Bonfil and S. Bowman dealing with the role of midrash in medieval Jewish historiography. On the *Sitz im Leben* of the *Chronicles of Solomon bar Simson,* see now the suggestion of G. Cohen, "The Hebrew Crusade Chronicle and the Ashkenazi Tradition," in *Minḥah le-Naḥum: Biblical and Other Studies in Honor of Nahum M. Sarna,* ed. M. Fishbane and M. Brettler (Sheffield: Sheffield Academic Press, 1993), 36–53.

38. See Reeg, *Geschichte von den zehn Märtyrern,* 19*, 29*; cf. 43*.

39. For the passage as a whole, see the Introduction.

40. *Yosef 'Ometz* (Frankfurt-am-Main: Hermon, 1922), no. 482.

41. Ibid., no. 485.

42. See J. Katz, in his influential essay "Beyn TaTeNU le-TaH – TaT," in *Yitzḥak Baer Jubilee Volume,* ed. S. Baron (Jerusalem: Historical Society of Israel, 1960), 318–37.

43. See the sources mentioned on p. 64 and in n. 18; *Tos. Baba Qama* 91*a*, s.v. *ve-lo'; Pisqei Tosaphot, Baba Qama Ha-Ḥovel,* no. 215; Maimonides, *Mishneh Torah, Hilkhot Yesodei Ha-Torah* V.6–7.

44. *Yosef 'Ometz,* no. 486.

45. The *Yevein Metzula* chronicle was first printed in Venice in 1653 and was printed repeatedly thereafter. The popular Lvov edition, 1851, is unpaginated; the present episode occurs on 7*a*. On this theme, cf. the defiant resistance of R. Samson ben Pesaḥ of Ostropol, one of the martyrs of the Chmielnicki persecutions (1648). See the penetrating analysis of this saint's life and death by Y. Liebes, "Mysticism and Reality: Towards a Portrait of the Martyr and Kabbalist, R. Samson Ostropoler," in *Jewish Thought in the Seventeenth Century,* ed. I. Twersky and B. Septimus (Cambridge, Mass.: Harvard University Press, 1987), 221–55.

46. *Yosef 'Ometz,* no. 485.

47. See *Zohar* I.66*a*, 224*a–b*; III.69*a*. On the subject of metempsychosis, see G. Scholem, "Ḥaluqa De-Rabbanan," *Tarbiz* 24 (1955): 297–306.

48. The Kabbalistic tradition to which Hahn refers can be traced to Nachmanides and (his follower) Rabbeinu Baḥye in

the thirteenth century and their discussion of how Abraham observed all 613 commandments *before* Sinai. Fuller considerations of the topic occur in the sixteenth century, particularly in the *Shnei Lukhot Ha-Berit* of R. Isaiah Horowitz, where the discussion is extended to consider how an observantly minded Jew could perform commandments that applied to earlier times (the Temple period) or special places (the land of Israel). Overall, see A. Green, *Devotion and Commandment: The Faith of Abraham in the Hasidic Imagination* (Cincinnati: Hebrew Union College Press, 1989), 38–48. I shall return to this point in the next chapter.

49. Meir ibn Gabbai, *'Avodat ha-Qodesh* (Venice, 1567), pt. IV (*Sitrei Torah*), chap. 36 (end).

50. *Zohar* II.124b.

51. *Songs Rabba* 1.2.xv; see above, pp. 19–20.

52. *'Arvei Naḥal*, vol. II, *Parashat Mas'ei* (Piotrkow, 1888), 59b; also noted by N. Polen, "Ecstasy and Sanctification," *Kabbalah: A Newsletter of Current Research in Jewish Mysticism* 3.1 (1988): 8.

53. In the *'Arvei Naḥal* the two versions are conflated.

54. Again, the passage conflates the talmudic episodes, since Akiba's companions only appear in *b. Berakhot* 61b.

55. R. Eybeschuetz studied with R. Meshullam Phoebus of Zbarazh and others of the Maggid's school. Note also the emphasis on the realm of Thought here and the discourse of the Maggid discussed at the end of the previous chapter.

56. *Midrash 'Eikha Rabba* I.16 (ed. S. Buber [Vilna, 1899], 42b); cf. *b. Giṭṭin* 58a.

57. *b. Yoma* 54a.

58. *Di Yudishe Melukhe un Andre Zakhen* (New York: Idish Leben, 1929). I learned of this story from D. Roskies, *Against the Apocalypse* (Cambridge, Mass.: Harvard University Press, 1984), 149–50.

3. *"As if he sacrificed a soul"*
Forms of Ritual Simulation and Substitution

1. See Introduction, pp. 5–8.

2. See chapter 2, pp. 75–77.

3. *b. Berakhot* 17a.

4. *Midrash Leviticus Rabba* III. 5 (end) (ed. M. Margoliot, 2d ed. [Jerusalem: Wahrmann Books, 1973], 1:68). Here Leviticus 2:1, "A person [soul] who offers a meal-offering to the Lord," is rearranged and parsed to mean "If one were to offer his [or her] soul, that would be like a meal-offering to the Lord." For a discussion of this passage within the larger thematics of the homily in Parasha 3, see N. J. Cohen, "Leviticus Rabbah, Parasha 3: An Example of a Classic Rabbinic Homily," *Jewish Quarterly Review* 72 (1981): 18–31, esp. pp. 26–27.

5. *M. Nega'im* II. 1. The rest of his remark goes, "For indeed they [the 'bright spots' being discussed] are like boxwood [*'eshkero'a*], [which is] not dark and not white but intermediate." The formulation puns on the word *'eshkero'a,* since this noun suggests the (pausal) verbal form "I shall be humbled"! For Rabbi Ishmael's formula, compare the popular cry whereby the people comfort a high priest in mourning (*M. Sanhedrin* II. 1).

6. *M. Sanhedrin* VI. 2. Rabbi Judah then proposed another formulation for a person who alleged that he was the victim of an evidentiary conspiracy, but his colleagues rightly rebutted his suggestion.

7. See *Tosefta: Mo'ed, Massekhet Kippurim* IV.6–8 (ed. S. Lieberman [New York: Jewish Theological Seminary of America, 1962), 252–53; and with a slight variation, *Mekhilta de-Rabbi Ishmael, Ba-Ḥodesh* VII (Horowitz-Rabin edition, p. 228).

8. The common reading in the *Mekhilta* is *she-meḥallel,* for "desecrate," with the variant (Oxford manuscript) *she-nitḥallel;* the latter is common to *Tosefta.* More significantly, the *Tosefta* adds the qualifier that the desecration be done "intentionally" (*mezid*), though this is absent in the Erfurt and London manuscripts (see *Tosefta: Mo'ed, Massekhet Kippurim,* Lieberman's apparatus to line 41; and his comment in *Tosefta Ki-Feshuṭa,* IV, *Seder Mo'ed* [New York: Jewish Theological Seminary, 1962], 824) and *Mekhilta.*

9. *Tosefta: Mo'ed, Massekhet Kippurim* IV.6–8 (Lieberman edition, pp. 252–53). For the idea that a martyr's death serves as expiation, see *Sifrei Deuteronomy* 333 (Finkelstein edition, p. 383).

10. *Shirei Levi ibn Altaban,* ed. D. Pagis (Jerusalem: Israel Academy of Sciences and Humanities, 1968), 68–69.

11. In "Prayer Book for the Liturgical Year with the '*Etz*

Ḥayyim' Commentary of R. Y. Tzalaḥ" (Jerusalem, 1894), 2:81; cited in *Mi-Ginzei Shirat ha-Qedem,* Y. Ratzaby (Jerusalem: Misgav Yerushalayim, 1991), 272.

12. *Shirei Qodesh,* ed. D. Yarden (Jerusalem, 1971), 184. I have rendered *mey resisekha,* "the waters of Your dew," freely as "healing waters" since divine dew is a common trope for healing or resurrection.

13. *Shirei Qodesh le-Rabbi Shlomo ben Yehuda ibn Gabirol,* ed. Bialik and Ravnitzky, 106.

14. *Sefer ha-Manhig,* ed. Y. Raphael (Jerusalem: Mosad Ha-Rav Kook, 1978), I (*dinei tefillah* 1), 36–37 (Hebrew pagination); the ruling follows *Sefer ha-'Orah* (par. 12): *qorban ḥashvinan le-hu* (note to line 36). The scriptural citation from Hosea is remarkable: although it accords with the main sense of the Massoretic text, the reading *peri* (fruit) instead of *parim* (bulls) is similar to the Septuagint *karpon* (fruit).

15. *Abudarham ha-Shallem* (Jerusalem: Usha, 1959), *seder shaḥarit shel ḥol,* 48.

16. *Sefer Shibbolei ha-Leqeṭ ha-Shalem,* ed. S. Buber (Vilna, 1886), 2. R. Zedekiah's brother, R. Benjamin, is cited as having written "that the recitation of the *tamid*-service is obligatory [*ḥovah*]."

17. *Perushei Siddur ha-Tefillah la-Rokeaḥ,* ed. R. Moshe Hirschler and R. Yehudah Alter Hirschler (Jerusalem: Makhon Ha-Rav Hirschler, 1992), 1:26; on p. 35 R. Eleazar justifies the custom by citations from Hosea 14:3 and *b. Megillah* 31*b*.

18. *Shulḥan 'Arukh, 'Oraḥ Ḥayyim,* I.

19. Isaiah Horowitz, *Shnei Lukhot ha-Berit,* vol. 2, pt. 1 (*Torah She-Bikhtav*), 1*c–d*.

20. Ibid.; and see the discussion of this source and older sources in Green, *Devotion and Commandment.*

21. *Shnei Lukhot ha-Berit,* vol. 2, pt. 1, 1*d*.

22. Ibid., vol. 1, pt. 2 (*Ta'anit, Me'inyan ha-'Avodah*), 45*a*.

23. Ibid., vol. 2, pt. 2 (*Torah She-Be'al Peh*), 23*b*. A variation of this recitation, in a more condensed form, recurs in R. Nathan Neta Hanover's slightly later (1662) collection of prayers called *Sha'arei Tziyyon;* see the Pisa, 1789, edition, 95*a*-96*a*. The *SHeLaH* was first published in Amsterdam in 1649.

24. Scholem noted the ideological link in *Kirjath Sefer* 7 (1930–31): 441 (see above, chapter 2, n. 6).

25. *The Book of the Pomegranate: Moses de Leon's Sefer ha-Rimmon,* ed. E. R. Wolfson (Atlanta: Scholars Press, 1988), 225–26.

26. This is a further argument against Katz's position, discussed earlier, pp. 74–77.

27. See above, pp. 44–45, 76, 79–80.

28. *Book of the Pomegranate,* 41–42.

29. Ibid., 39–40.

30. Ibid., 43–44; the earlier reference to joy is at pp. 37–38.

31. *Bayit Ḥadash* to *Ṭur, 'Oraḥ Ḥayyim,* sec. 61.

32. Eliezer Azikri, *Sefer Ḥaredim* (Zolkiew, 1804), 20*b*.

33. See above, pp. 91–92, and nn. 7–9.

34. The rite is not performed during Sabbath and Holy Festivals, certain minor feast days and fasts, and various other occasions varying from a day to a month, depending upon custom. These times are listed in the Codes, like the *Shulḥan 'Arukh, 'Oraḥ Ḥayyim,* 131.5–7, and in collections of local practice, like the *Keter Shem Ṭov* by Shem Ṭov Gagin, which gives the Sephardi rites of London, Amsterdam, and Israel. The specifics of the practice and its explanations appear in these texts, old prayer books (e.g., the *Siddur Rav Amram Gaon* and the *Maḥzor Vitry*), and collections of practices (e.g., the *Shibbolei ha-Leqeṭ*).

35. See simply the gloss of R. Moses Isserles to the *Shulḥan 'Arukh, 'Oraḥ Ḥayyim,* 131.1. The Sephardi practice is noted there; and the many reasons for the changes in orientation are found in the literature mentioned in the previous note and elsewhere.

36. It is noteworthy that in thirteenth-century Ashkenaz the Rokeaḥ teaches the recitation of Psalm 25 during the *nefilat 'appayim* rite; see his *Perushei Siddur ha-Tefillah* (Hirschler and Hirschler edition), 2:395; but on p. 405 he comments that "some say" Psalm 3.

37. *Rabbeinu Baḥye: Be'ur 'al ha-Torah,* ed. H. D. Chavel (Jerusalem: Mosad Ha-Rav Kook, 1982), 3:115–17.

38. See also the comments of I. Tishby, *Mishnat ha-Zohar* (Jerusalem: Bialik Institute, 1976), 2:275.

39. There are six gradations of this masculine structure between the highest feminine grade (*Binah*), which is third from the top, and the lowest feminine grade (*Malkhut*), which is the tenth. Correspondingly, there are six key blessings which bracket the Amidah (three and three), and these form the "six

extremities" or "poles," which often symbolize the masculine principle (*Tiferet*).

40. This would seem to be the very zoharic passage alluded to by R. Abraham ben Eliezer in his *Megillat Amraphel*, discussed above.

41. *Zohar Hadash, Terumah*, ed. R. Margoliot (Jerusalem: Mosad Ha-Rav Kook, 1979), 42*a*.

42. Y. Liebes, *Ha-Mashiaḥ shel ha-Zohar*, in *Ha-Ra'ayon ha-Meshiḥiy be-Yiśrael* (Jerusalem: Israel Academy of Sciences and Humanities, 1982), 177–78, n. 311, makes the case for the demythologized *qof*. Wolfson (*Book of the Pomegranate*, 84, note to line 1) transfers his point to the larger issue of devotion of the self without being specific. The discussion of the missing letters appears in *Sefer ha-Rimmon*, Wolfson edition, pp. 84–85.

43. Moshe Cordovero, *Tefillah le-Moshe* (Przemysl, 1892), 107*b*, 110*b*–112*b*.

44. Ibid., 112*a*.

45. For the mythic background of *mayyin nuqvin* in rabbinic and zoharic traditions, see Liebes, *Ha-Mashiaḥ*, 179, n. 314.

46. Cordovero, *Tefillah le-Moshe*, 112*b*.

47. Yitzḥaq Luria, *Sha'ar ha-Kavvanot, 'Inyan Nefilat 'Appayim* (Jerusalem, 1989), 1:301*b*–314*b*. This work includes five interpretations of the rite.

48. See ibid., Interpretation (*Derush*) 1, 301*b*–302*a*.

49. The *Ze'ir 'Anpin* is the Lurianic equivalent of the six lower gradations (from *Tiferet* to *Yesod*), not including the final gradation of *Malkhut*, or the Shekhinah. In *Ze'ir 'Anpin* the divine qualities of mercy, justice, and compassion are in balance.

50. See the whole discussion in Luria, *Sha'ar ha-Kavvanot*, *Derush* 2, 302*a*–305*a*.

51. See ibid., *Derush* 3, 305*a*–307*b*.

52. See ibid., *Derush* 5, 310*b*–314*b*; and on *'Inyan Kavvanat Keriyat Shema*, see *Derush* 5, 137*b*.

53. This stasis is marked by the terms *dayyeqa'* and *mamash*, "precisely"; see ibid., 137*b*.

54. Here, too, the key term *'aleykha* is marked by *dayyeqa'* and *mamash*; see ibid., 137*b* and 310*a*.

55. See above, p. 82.

56. See above, p. 83.

57. The lower syzygy of kisses is also effected by the (silent)

recitation of a doxology that immediately follows the Shema ("Blessed be His glorious Kingdom for ever and ever"), which mentions the glory of God's *Malkhut,* or Kingdom; and also by the person of Moses, who spoke with God "mouth to mouth" – that is, spirit to spirit (the zoharic way of talking about a syzygy between *Tiferet* and *Malkhut; Zohar* II.124*b*).

58. Cf. op. cit., 312*a-b.*

59. *Qunṭeres ha-Hitpa'alut* is published under the title *Liqquṭei Be'urim* (Warsaw, 1868), which includes the text with a commentary by Rabbi Hillel of Paritch.

60. *Liqquṭei Be'urim,* 54*b.*

61. See the brief but penetrating discussion of this and other levels in N. Loewenthal, *Communicating the Infinite: The Emergence of the Habad School* (Chicago: University of Chicago Press, 1990), 124–31.

62. *Liqquṭei Be'urim,* 55*b.*

63. Ibid., 56*a.*

64. *Sha'ar ha-Teshuvah veha-Tefillah* was published in two parts in Shklov (1817 and 1818); it was reprinted as one volume entitled *Sha'arei Teshuvah* (Zhitomer, 1864). I have used the later edition (reprint, Brooklyn, 1983), where part I is *Sha'arei Tefillah.* For an earlier examination of *nefilat 'appayim* in this work, see the discussion of N. Lowenstein, "Self-sacrifice of the Zaddik in the Teachings of R. Dov Ber, the *Mittler Rebbe,*" in *Jewish History: Essays in Honor of Chimen Abramsky,* ed. A. Rapaport-Albert and S. Zipperstein (London: P. Halban, 1988), 465–71. His larger concern is with the central role of self-sacrifice in early Hasidic thought; see also Loewenthal, *Communicating the Infinite,* 55–56, 90–97, 127–28.

65. *Sha'arei Teshuvah,* I.42*b*–43*b*; the verse is cited again at 44*a* and 47*a,* where the exegesis is developed. It seems that Dov Ber was strongly influenced by his father, R. Shneur Zalman, who in his *Seder Tefillot* (Kopyst, 1831; 4th ed., Brooklyn, 1986), 21*a,* begins with the same proof text and distinguishes the superiority of the *nefilat 'appayim* ritual from the ecstatic states to be achieved during the recital of the Shema and the Amidah. Dov Ber follows his father's reasons for this (and the terms), although he goes a bit farther in his analyses. Several other important borrowings from his father will be pointed out below (see nn. 66–67, 70–71).

This filiation of ideas was not recognized in Loewenthal's consideration.

66. Shneur Zalman, *Seder Tefillot*, 81c–82d, treats at length the theme of "astonishment" from Genesis 24:21 as the basis of being opened to a new (initial) level of spiritual consciousness. Dov Ber follows him in this and in one of the analogies.

67. Shneur Zalman, ibid., 26a, uses the image of glue in connection with spiritual bonding; and he strikingly reuses Ezekiel 37:17, *ve-hayu le-'ahadim mamash* ("they shall be One in actuality"), 26d (var., 26a), to convey the *unio mystica* involved. He also speaks of the mystical state as one of absorption, saying, "when the soul and body are totally absorbed [*be-hikkalel*] in the Unity of God, they shall be One in actuality."

68. *Sha'arei Teshuvah*, 45c; here and elsewhere the term *mamash* is repeated, often in conjunction with the recitation of Psalm 25. This derives from Lurianic models; see above, p. 114, and nn. 53–54.

69. Ibid., 45d–46c.

70. Ibid., 46c–d. See also Shneur Zalman, *Seder Tefillot*, 26a–d, where the oxymoron of being "as if" (*ke'ilu*) dead and "actually" (*mamash*) dead is developed to show that in the *nefilat 'appayim* rite one actualizes martyrdom and achieves a truer level of adhesion to God.

71. *Sha'arei Teshuvah*, 47a and esp. 45d. Shneur Zalman, *Seder Tefillot*, 26a, already makes the point.

72. See the discussion of Maimonides, above, pp. 29–30; and the important comment of Nahmanides on Deuteronomy 11:22.

73. This is strongly put in Rabbi Aaron's *'Avodat ha-Levi* (Lemberg, 1862), *Tetzaveh*, fol. 47c. For a wider discussion of Rabbi Aaron's views on *nefilat 'appayim*, see Rachel Elior, *Torat ha-'Elohut be-Dor Sheni shel Hasidut HaBaD* (Jerusalem: Magnes Press, 1982), 273–81; and for the issues between him and Dov Ber, see Loewenthal, *Communicating the Infinite*, chap. 4.

74. *Sha'arei Teshuvah*, I.47a.

75. Shabbetai Sheftel Horowitz, in his gloss to *Shenei Lukhot ha-Berit*, vol. 1, pt. 2 (*Massekhet Pesahim*), 4b–c. In his *Sha'arei Tziyyon*, 104a–b, Hanover also elaborates on the New Moon period as a time for atonement, and notes pertinent prayers.

76. See *Sha'arei Tziyyon*, I, pt. 2, 165b–166b.

77. Naftali Katz, *Sefer ha-Hakhanah* (Constantinople, 1744), 17*b*.

78. Cf. *Sefer ha-Hakhanah*.

79. Cf. *b. Yevamot* 105*b*.

80. See R. Ḥayyim Viṭal, *Sha'arei Qedushah* III.8 (and the discussion above, pp. 44–45); also R. Eliezer Azikri, *Sefer Ḥaredim*, 68*a*. The advice of R. Shabbetai Sheftel should thus be added to sources collected by Idel in "Ha-Hitboddedut" (see above, chap. 1, n. 67), 79–81, and Z. Gries, *Sifrut ha-Hanhagot* (Jerusalem: Mosad Bialik, 1989), 220–22.

81. The text is found at the beginning of Rabbi Elimelekh's *No'am 'Elimelekh* (Cracow, 1896) and in collections of spiritual practices.

Index

Index

Index

Index